On Your Own

Navigating the Road to Independence

D1157376

JoAnn Jumper

On Your Own: Navigating the Road to Independence

Published by Wheatmark®
2030 East Speedway Boulevard, Suite 106
Tucson, Arizona 85719 USA
www.wheatmark.com

International Standard Book Number: 978-1-60494-251-4
Library of Congress Control Number: 2009921467

Interior and back cover illustrations by Brittan Jumper.

rev20100115
rev201803

Acknowledgments

I want to express my deepest appreciation to my amazing husband of forty-nine years, David, who suggested the authoring of this book and who has continued to provide support, encouragement, and suggestions throughout the entire process, as he has done with all of my endeavors.

My sincere appreciation goes to my children and their spouses, who have likewise encouraged me throughout this project. In particular, I thank Russell for his editing and Brittan for her imagination, creativity, and artwork in this book. I am very appreciative to Rachel, Wes, Clint and Renee for their contributions and support. I am also grateful to Janet, Greg, and Jordan for their contributions to the concept and process. Everyone's suggestions and ideas have been a tremendous asset to the development of this manuscript.

My thanks to Grael Norton and Lori Conser at Wheatmark Publishing as well, for so patiently answering questions and guiding me through the publication process.

I would like to dedicate this book to Kristen, who was the inspiration for this book, and to Owen, Grant, Addison, Reese, Austin, Kate, Caroline, Luke, and Wyatt, my grandchildren. I cannot wait to encourage and support each of you on your journey to independence!

Table of Contents

Alcohol
Drugs
Sex and Pregnancy

Introduction

The future depends on what you do today.
— Mahatma Gandhi

All of your life you have been preparing for this journey toward independence. From the moment you arrived on this Earth, you have been learning to talk, walk, manage relationships with parents and friends, and deal with issues at school. You have probably learned many things about how to do homework, and how to handle problems with friends, but perhaps the most important thing you have learned is that you are in the driver's seat, and that only *you* are in charge of your journey through life.

There are many keys to developing life skills, some of which you may have already discovered. Often times, however, the most important keys are overlooked or are not thoroughly taught or learned. This book will introduce you to additional skills that will make your life journey easier and more successful.

This book is designed to help you navigate through your life journey in such a way that the trip is as successful as possible, avoiding many of the potholes, speed bumps, and collisions you might encounter in life as you travel.

There is information throughout the book marked as:

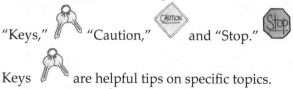

"Keys,"   "Caution,"   and "Stop."

Keys   are helpful tips on specific topics.

Caution signs   indicate information to consider before you proceed. You may want to research and evaluate this information or discuss it with a trusted friend before you follow a certain path.

Stop signs   indicate information or situations you will *definitely* want to evaluate further or completely avoid. These will be helpful as you learn how to manage a budget, rent an apartment, apply for a job, etc.

Each chapter is self-contained for easy reference to the particular subject in which you are interested. By preparing well for your journey you may avoid many of the road hazards and speed bumps that some people encounter as they begin their journey through life. I wish you the smoothest ride possible as you proceed *On Your Own*.

1

Managing Finances

> *I am not a product of my circumstances.*
> *I am a product of my decisions.*
>
> — Stephen Covey

The majority of people, when they are on their own, find that one of the most critical steps to success is efficiently managing their finances. Money fuels the engine of your car to begin your journey to independence. To ensure that your journey is as successful as possible, your engine must be running well enough to continue your trip and to get you where you want to go. No matter where your destination may be, you must have enough fuel to reach your destination.

Budgeting

Keeping a budget will ensure that you have the fuel to arrive where you want to be.

People are different from one another in all areas of their lives, but successful individuals have one thing in common: the ability to manage their money well. Budgeting is a tool used by most successful people. It does not matter how much money you have. A budget will help you manage whatever money you do have so that you have enough to pay your rent, put gas in your car, buy groceries, and provide for the other necessities of life. Budgeting will also help you handle emergencies by leaving you enough money to meet unexpected expenses. There *will* be emergencies. Dealing with unexpected expenses such as flat tires, gifts, travel, and medical needs is a fact of life.

You will have to be disciplined and committed to make a budget work for you.

There are several approaches to budgeting. Below is the process I like to use.

Step 1- List all of the routine expenses you expect to have each month, including the amount of money you decide to put into savings.

Putting money into savings each month, even if it is just $5.oo a month, will help you begin the healthy habit of saving. It will be very helpful to have money in savings for those times when your car breaks down or you need a new refrigerator.

Some likely categories of expenses for your budget are:

- Savings (or emergency funds)
- Rent (housing)
- Utilities (gas, water, electric, cable)
- Car payment
- Gasoline
- Groceries
- Eating out
- Clothing
- Entertainment
- Insurance (renters and/or auto)
- Medical expenses
- Miscellaneous expenses

At least 10 percent of your income should be set aside for emergency expenses.

Step 2- Estimate the amount of money you expect to spend each month in each category. Try to remember what things you have spent money on in the last month. Make a list of these items and the amount of money you spent for each. You will probably see a pattern develop and that will help you decide what categories of spending you will want to include in your budget and how much money you think you should estimate for each category. Put your estimated spending beside each category on your budget sheet for easy reference.

CAUTION

If this is the first time you have lived on your own and established a budget, it is a good idea to go to the grocery store and check the prices of the items you frequently buy. This will help you determine how much money you will need for groceries and personal items.

CAUTION

Checking the rental ads online or in the newspaper for apartment costs in the area in which you want to live will help with establishing your budget.

Don't forget to put the anticipated expenses in each of these categories of your budget sheet. (See an example below.)

Budget	Savings-$5	Rent-$250	Food-$300	Gas-$75
January				
February				
March				
April				
May				
June				
July				
August				
September				
October				
November				
December				

Step 3- For the next month or two keep a notebook with you and list everything you spend for each month. This should help you begin to determine an accurate record of how much money you actually spend each month. You may find that you spend more money in some categories and less in others than you estimated.

CAUTION The records you keep for that month should include every purchase you make, even soft drinks purchased at the convenience store, and other inexpensive items you bought so that you can track where you are spending your money.

Step 4- At the end of the month enter the actual amount you spent in each of your categories for that month.

Stop If you have payments that are due annually or semi-annually you might find it helpful to place an asterisk in the month in which the payment is due. Then place a note at the bottom of your budget sheet to remind yourself of what payment is due and the amount of the payment.

CAUTION Documenting all expenses you had helps you make a much more realistic budget and helps you see where you may be spending money frivolously.

Step 5- Once you have recorded all of your expenses, review your budget and make adjustments. Did you allow enough in each category for what you spent?

Did you allow too much? Do the categories reflect your spending correctly?

After two to three months you will begin to see patterns in your budget. Most people find they allowed too much money in one category and not enough in another. Now is the time to make adjustments in the necessary categories so that your budget is accurate and reasonable.

Once you establish a budget that you feel is accurate, you will feel much more comfortable with how you spend your money and feel more in control of it.

It is a good idea to review your budget every three to six months so that you can make appropriate, realistic adjustments.

Whenever possible increase the amount of money you are putting into your savings account.

There are several online budgeting tools that you may find helpful in managing your budget. You can google "online budgeting tools" and see several suggestions. Some online budgeting tools are easy to use and well designed. They help you keep up with finances, transactions, investments, and other financial information. Some of the sites you might find helpful are Mint.com, PersonalCapital.com, Tiller.com and QuickBooks.com. It is important to search several sites before choosing the tool you want to use as they all vary in the information with which they help, the page layouts, and how they allow the user to interact with the site.

Some of the online tools are free to use and others have fees associated with their use. Be sure to check for any fees connected to the tool you find that fits your needs before choosing a site so that you do not have any surprises.

Keeping receipts for expenses is also a good idea even though you may also be storing that information on your smart phone. If you have kept receipts and your phone crashes, you will have a backup record for your reference. An accordion folder or a file cabinet is a good place to store any paper receipts. Storage can be purchased at places like Wal-Mart, Target, or office supply stores.

Paychecks

Depending on where you work, you will receive a paycheck weekly, biweekly, or monthly. Your check will generally be deposited electronically into your checking account by your employer so it will be necessary for you to open a checking account at a bank or credit union. (I will talk about how to do this later in this chapter.)

Each check you earn will have a pay advice or pay stub attached. This is an explanation of your income and withdrawals that have been made from your check. Pay stubs or pay advices itemize all of the information related to your earnings. The pay stub generally reflects the number of hours you worked, your gross pay (the money earned before any deductions—twenty hours a week at $10 an hour is $200 gross), and any taxes or other deductions (i.e., insurance, retirement, federal withholding, and/or Social Security deductions) that are withdrawn from your gross pay.

Most employers will withhold some money from your paycheck for income taxes and the employer will use that money to pay the necessary taxes to the appropriate entities. Smaller companies and employers who pay your earnings in cash may expect you to be responsible for paying your own income taxes.

If you are responsible for calculating and paying your own taxes you may want to seek assistance from a professional (perhaps an accountant) who is knowledgeable about taxes.

Once you know what your net pay will be, you will determine how to pay your bills based on how often you are paid (weekly, biweekly, or monthly). If you receive a weekly paycheck, you will need to decide which bills you must pay the first week of the month—generally that will be rent or housing expenses—and which bills you will pay each of the other weeks.

If you are spending more than you budgeted in certain parts of your budget, it is critical that you adjust your spending to keep from running out of money and creating debt.

When you pay each bill it is a good idea to write the date you made the payment, the amount of the payment, and the method of payment (online confirmation number, check or money order number) on the part of the bill you keep as your receipt. If you ever have to verify payment you will have an easy way to check your method of payment and the date that the payment was made.

There are several ways to organize receipts. One way to is to file the receipts in a manila file folder labeled with the name of the company (Urban Outfitter, the Gap) or the type of payment (rent, utilities, gas). Another way is to use a file for each month of the year. Put all of January's receipts in a folder labeled January, February's receipts in a file labeled February, etc. If you choose to file by the month, when January rolls around again, you can discard most receipts from January of the previous year. Receipts for items that are big purchases or ongoing payments, like car payments or credit card payments, should be kept for the entire time you are making the payments or, in some cases, longer.

If you decide not to open a bank account into which your check will be deposited, it will be just as important to manage the money you have. You may need to ask your employer to pay you in person with an actual written check. There should also be a pay advice or pay stub attached to your check.

Once you cash your paycheck it is a good idea to have envelopes marked for each of the categories in your budget (rent, food, etc.). You can divide the cash into the amounts you have determined sufficient for each budgeted item. By doing this you can be sure that the rent money is not spent for entertainment or something else. Arrange the envelopes in alphabetical order and keep them in a box or container similar to a receipt or photo box. This, of course, needs to be stored in a safe place.

It is a good idea to keep a folded $20.00 bill in your wallet that you never intend to spend. That way when an emergency arises and you are out of cash, you will always be able to make calls, purchase food, or buy a little gas. As your income increases replace the $20.00 bill with a $50.00 bill and eventually a $100.00 bill. You will be amazed at what this will do for your self-confidence!

Paying Bills

When you receive your hard-earned paycheck there are several ways you can manage your money. You may decide to open a checking account and/or savings account at a local bank. Once you open an account, you can use your smartphone, tablet and/or computer, or obtain a mobile app from your banking institution to manage your money. Or you may choose to write checks to pay bills.

A very convenient way of paying bills is through Auto-pay. In order to do this you must have a credit card or checking account. Many businesses accept auto-pay and it is very easy for the consumer to pay their bill.

If you decide you want to use auto-pay you must contact the company to which the payment will go. They will set up your account so that your bill will be paid each month by an automatic charge on your credit card or by the provider automatically drafting the amount of the payment out of your checking account. Once your card is charged or your account is drafted, you will receive notification as to the amount that has been charged to your credit card or drawn out of your account.

With any electronic or online options of managing your money, you will need a user name and password to manage that account.

Be sure that you create a difficult password for your accounts. Most difficult passwords generally contain letters (with some capitalized), numbers, and signs in nonsensical combinations. Your password needs to be something you can remember but would be difficult for others to figure out. Do not use your birthdate, mother's maiden name and other identifying information that is easy for thieves to obtain.

Whether you choose an electronic option to manage your money or you decide to use checks, you will find many tools to help you. Some of these tools are available through your financial institution and others can be found online. You can track your spending, set goals, or have funds automatically sent to savings. You may categorize how you spend your money, have notifications of changes to your account sent to you, and/or set up date reminders of regular expenses you have such as rent, car payment, insurance, etc.

Some programs will sort your transactions based on your budget categories. Some options will also show you your average spending and send notifications if you have spent more money than you allocated in a certain category. You can use as few or as many options available as you choose. The real convenience with internet banking is that you can manage your account any time day or night.

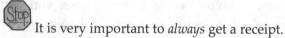 If you choose online options to manage your money, be SURE you have a secure password,. Change your password every few months, and DO NOT share your password with anyone.

If you choose to write checks instead of using online banking, it is critical that you keep accurate written records of your spending.

Another option for paying bills is to purchase money orders with cash. You may also choose to cash your checks and use only cash to pay bills.

It is very important to *always* get a receipt.

Some receipts are printed on paper that fades over time. If your receipt is for an expensive or important item, be sure to make a copy of the receipt and store the copy with the receipt.

If you are paying with cash, you will need to go to each creditor in person to deliver your payment.

You will need to allow money for transportation if you decide to pay your bills in person.

If you choose to pay your bills with money orders you must go to a convenience store, bank, or post office and purchase the money orders with cash. Money orders guarantee that the money will be paid to the person to whom you address the money order. You will have to fill out the name and address of the person you wish to receive the money. When you complete the money order record the recipient, the date, and the amount of the money order on the attached stub. There will be a fee charged for each money order you purchase. This fee is generally determined by the value of the money order.

It is important to file the money order receipt with your other receipts in case the money order is lost in the mail or stolen.

If the money order is lost, you can take your

receipt to the location where you purchased it, and they will be able to verify whether or not the money order was actually cashed. If the money order has been cashed, but not by the intended recipient, it will be important for you to notify the police.

Checking/Savings Accounts

If you decide to open a checking and/or savings account you will first need to select a bank or credit union. Most financial institutions will have a branch location that is convenient to the parts of town where you live, work, or go to school.

All banks and credit unions have customer service representatives who can advise you as to what types of accounts are best for you. These representatives will make you aware of various fees and minimum balance requirements that are associated with the various accounts. They will also inform you of the automated calling systems and internet banking options that are available.

When opening an account, you only have one opportunity to make a first impression! Dress in clothing that is neat and clean. You want to leave the impression that you are ready to handle the important task of managing your finances.

In order to open an account you will need to fill out an application and provide a driver's license, Social Security card, and a certain amount of money. Depending on your age and/or credit history the bank may want someone to cosign on your bank account. The bank will expect the cosigner to take care of any expenses associated with your account if you are unable to do so. This person should be someone who is financially sound and whom you trust to help with this very important responsibility. If you make a mistake and do not have sufficient funds in your bank account to cover a check (making it a "hot check"), then your cosigner will have to cover your check if you are unable to.

Some banks offer overdraft protection and will cover your check if enough money is not in your checking account, but is in your savings account. Be sure to ask about this service.

Savings accounts are also available at the bank and are a great place to keep emergency funds. If you request it, some banks will automatically take an amount you designate from any deposits you make and put that amount directly into your savings account while the remainder of your deposit will go into your checking account.

Money Management Tools

Online budgeting tools are mentioned above in the budgeting section. Financial institutions also offer many ways by which you can manage your money. Most people rely on some form of electronic service as a way to access their accounts and manage their money. This is very convenient as access to your account can be by use of a computer, tablet, smartphone or app. With these tools, you can access your account any time 24/7.

Some of the services available through your financial institution include the viewing of electronic bank statements, sorting your spending into different categories, viewing your average monthly spending, and due date reminders. Every financial institution is a little different in terms of the services available so be sure to ask about available services and select a financial institution that offers the services you are interested in using. You may use as many of the available services as you would like.

If you prefer, your bank may also have apps that will help you manage your money. These apps offer many of the services that the financial institutions offer.

There are also apps and online tools that allow you to transfer money from one person to another if you both have the same app. This might be convenient if you are sharing an apartment and wish to split the rent or are out to eat and wish to pay for your part of the bill by electronically transferring money to one of your friends. Some apps also keep a history of your transactions. Two apps you might want to explore for sending money to others are Venmo.com and Pay-Pal.com.

CAUTION   Be sure to check on whether or not there are fees or minimum balances associated with accounts and apps before signing up for a particular service or app.

There may also be a limit as to how many times a week or a month you may use this service.

Before selecting internet options, be sure that you are comfortable with the security features of your choice.

Keep in mind that someone who chooses to send you a payment electronically can also stop payment on the transaction if they choose.

Some apps offer options in which you can actually view your friends spending. I strongly caution that you do NOT choose to do that. You may make your information private rather than public to prevent the opportunity of someone tracking your actions.

If you are not interested in using internet features with your account, you can maintain a check book and check register. (Details are below.)

Whether you use an internet method or write checks to pay bills, you will find that some banks will require a $25 minimum balance in your account. Some banks may require more. Most banks provide several types of checking and savings accounts. Some will have fees associated with the accounts—for instance, a small charge of $3.00 to $5.00 if your account balance dips below $500 or a designated amount. If you believe it will be difficult for you to maintain the required balance in your account, ask about accounts that do not include these associated fees. Some banks have special accounts that they offer to individuals in specific circumstances, like students who are enrolled in school.

There is generally a substantial fee if you write a check for more than the amount of money that is in your bank account. This may be as much as $50.00 or more.

If you decide to pay your bills by checks, and do not have sufficient funds in your account, there may also be a charge assessed by the bank of the person to whom you have given a bad check. These fees can add up quickly, so be sure to keep good records.

Using checks requires that you will have certain personal information printed on your checks. Many people do not use first names, but instead use first and/or middle initials and last names to reduce the possibility of being a victim of identity theft.

Do not have your driver's license or Social Security number printed on your checks. That information makes it easier for someone to steal your identity.

Once you order your checks, it will take approximately a week to receive them through the mail. The bank will give you temporary checks to use, if necessary, until your permanent checks arrive. When you receive your permanent checks, you will also get a record-keeping booklet called a check register. You should immediately enter the amount of money deposited at the bank to open your account in the column marked "Deposit," and then write that amount in the far right column labeled "Balance."

If you have used any temporary checks, write the number of each check and the name of the recipient. Also enter the amount of each check in the column marked "payment" and subtract your entry from the balance. Put the new balance in the column labeled "balance". This way you will always know how much money is available in your account. At the end of each month, the bank will send you a statement showing deposits and expenses; you can also check this information online. Always review this statement and compare the deposits and checks that the bank shows you have written to the records you have made in your check register.

Each time you write a check or make a deposit, it is imperative that you write down the date, the name of the person or company to whom you wrote the check, and the amount of the check so that you always know the amount of money remaining in your checking account.

Watch for any additional bank fees on your statement that you have not deducted from your balance and for any errors in the statement. Should an error occur, you can visit with a customer service representative at your bank for assistance with correcting the discrepancy.

Establishing Credit

Good credit is extremely valuable as you continue your journey down the road of life. People who consider doing business with you, renting apartments to you, and hiring you will check to see that you have good credit. Good credit shows that you have been responsible by paying your creditors (the people selling or renting to you) on time and in full. Employers feel that if you are responsible with your money, you are likely to be a good employee as well.

There are three credit reporting agencies that maintain credit histories on individuals. These reports show what type of credit an individual has maintained. Generally, individuals are allowed one free copy of their credit report each year. If you wish to obtain more than one, there will be a charge for that.

Just as you check the tires on your car to ensure they are safe, it is important to check your credit report to ensure that the information the credit bureaus have on record about you is accurate. On occasion, there can be mistakes in the information reported. You will not be aware of this unless you check your credit report regularly. You certainly do not want mistakes on your credit report as this could keep you from opening an account, renting an apartment, or getting a job.

The credit reporting agencies are Experian (1-888-397-3742, http://www.experian.com), Equifax Credit Information Service (1-800-685-1111, http://

www.equifax.com), and TransUnion Credit Bureau (1-800-916-8800, http://www.transunion.com).

If you are trying to rent an apartment or begin service for electricity, gas, phone, or internet, and you do not have any credit established, the provider may ask that you have an adult with a good credit rating cosign with you. As with your bank accounts, the cosigner would agree to be responsible for any bills you fail to pay. In addition, the providers of services may also require a deposit of $50 or more that they will keep and apply to your bill if you are unable to pay your bill.

Having a cosigner is one way to begin establishing credit. Another way is to apply for a credit card—only to establish credit—at a department store such as Sears or Wal-Mart. You can purchase an inexpensive item that you need and then pay the bill in full as soon as your bill arrives.

Be aware that there will be a cost to use these cards, typically $5.00 or so.

Creditors are interested in seeing that you pay your bills, not that you buy many items or very expensive items.

If you are a college student with limited financial resources you may find you need to ask your college or university to extend credit to you so you can make several smaller payments instead of one large one to the college for tuition and books. You would not want to have to postpone your education because of bad credit.

Buying a house or car may not be something you are ready to consider at this point, but someday it will be. Good credit is essential to purchasing more expensive items.

Almost all drivers have run out of gas once or twice. If for some reason your checkbook or bank account "runs out of gas" and you are unable to pay a bill or have to pay it late, it is very important to contact your creditor and explain the situation. Inform the creditor of when you expect to have the money to pay your your bill and tell them you will pay the bill the minute it arrives. Be SURE you pay that immediately. Most people will work with you if they can. If they do not hear from you, however, they will begin to feel you are irresponsible and might think that you will not pay their bill at all. The longer the bill goes unpaid before they hear from you the less likely they will be to work with you.

It is possible that the creditor will charge you extra interest (perhaps 5 to 6 percent of your debt) to give you extra time to pay your bill. The interest can add up in a hurry, so pay that bill as quickly as you can.

Credit Cards

Obtaining credit cards can be a major speed bump in life. Many very bright, well-educated people have used credit cards and then found they are unable to pay off the balance they charged to the credit card by the due date.

Opportunities to obtain credit cards are everywhere and will frequently fill your mailbox. It is awesome to think that someone out there wants to give you $1,000 or more in credit for just signing your name. The problem is that credit "given" to you needs to be repaid. Often the amount of money that you are required to pay on credit card debt does not seem like much. But by paying only the minimum amount due on the credit card each month, you will find that an item you purchased for $50 could actually cost several times that much due to the interest that accrues.

CAUTION Credit cards are useful in some situations but not recommended until you become very comfortable with managing your money and successfully paying your bills.

There may be situations in which it will be necessary for you use a credit card. Online purchases will generally require a credit card or debit card (see below). If you decide that a credit card is necessary, each time you charge an item enter the amount in your checkbook register as though you had written a check for that purchase. That way you have allotted the money in your bank account to pay for the credit card bill when it arrives. When you receive the bill, you can compare your check register with the credit card statement to be sure you have already deducted money for that charge. If you have already deducted each of the credit card purchases from your checking account, you are ready to write a check for the amount of your credit card bill.

If you have failed to deduct any purchases from your account, you will now need to do so in order to cover your payment to the credit card company.

There are credit card apps that will send you no-tifications whenever a charge has been made to your account. If the notification reflects a charge you did not make to your account, immediately contact your credit card company.

Do not sign the back of your credit card. Instead, write "See photo ID" or "Photo ID Required." This way, no one else is able to use your card.

It is a good idea to make a copy of the front and back of your card. Then if someone does wrongfully use it you have proof that you requested that your identity be confirmed by a photo ID.

If you decide to pay a bill online or by calling the company, be sure to request a confirmation number in case there is a problem with your transaction.

Check your credit card statement every few days to be sure there are no fraudulent charges. This can be done online. Remember that it may take several days for a charge to show up on your credit card statement.

Debit Cards

A debit card is another way to pay for purchases. Your bank or credit card company may issue one. When using a debit card you will need to enter a PIN (personal identification number) each time you use the card. The minute you use your debit card the amount of the transaction is removed from your bank account.

You might want to consider a reloadable debit card. You would place a certain amount of cash on the card in advance and then use the card to pay for items or services.

Some financial institutions and credit card companies charge a fee for each transaction on your debit card so be sure to ask about any fees related to the use of your card.

It is imperative that you know you have enough money in your account before attempting to use a debit card. Be sure to keep a record of debit expenditures so you always know the balance remaining in your account. This can be done electronically by viewing your account online.

It is a good idea to make a copy of the front and back of your debit card in case it is lost or stolen.

Micro Investing

Micro investing is a convenient way to begin saving money. With a debit card you are able to round up your purchases to the next dollar or make automatic transfers to a savings account.

Let's say you make a purchase for $3.40. The deduction from your debit card would be $4.00. The $.60 over the actual purchase amount of $3.40 would then be placed into your saving account.

This approach to investing will not make you rich, but will allow you to begin saving and over time will provide some money for small emergencies.

Some of the more popular micro investing apps are found at Acorn.com and Stash.com.

Loans

Even though many people do not like taking out loans, (and I do not recommend them) there may be a point in time when you need to consider this. I would only do this as a last resort when there may be an expense that occurs out of your control and you may find you do not have enough money in savings to cover this expense.

There are several ways you might borrow money. I would begin thinking about this situation by making a list of all possible people and places that might be willing to loan you money.

This list might include family, friends, and banks. Consider each option and determine if they will want to charge you interest (money on top of the loan amount that could be as much as 1% to 8% or more of the amount of money you need to borrow). If the lender will be charging you interest, this means if you borrow $1000 dollars, and the simple interest rate is 8%, you may be paying back a total of $1080 to complete paying off this debt.

There are several ways in which interest can be calculated. You will want to discuss this with your borrower so that you understand exactly how much it will cost to borrow money.

Simple interest and compound interest are the two primary types of interest charged. Be sure to clarify with your lender the approach they will be using and have the lender give you the TOTAL of what this loan will cost you when all fees are included.

Always have a written agreement with the person lending you money.

The agreement should include:

1.   the date of the agreement

2.   the amount of money you are borrowing

3.   if there is interest being charged and how much

4.   when payments will be made (weekly or monthly) and the amount of each payment

5.   the date the total amount is due

6.   signatures of both the lender and borrower

The lender and borrower should each retain a copy of this agreement. If you feel it is necessary, you can both go to a notary who will sign that he/she has witnessed both individuals signing the agreement.

Most banks, and city and county offices, have a public notary who will do this for you. There will be a fee assessed for their services.

People will often work with you to lend money, but they want you to fulfill the agreement you estab-lish. They do not like you coming back two or three times asking for an extension on the length of time in which you agreed to pay back their money.

Some people do not like to have family involved in their financial affairs and feel that it will be a strain on relationships to borrow money from family or friends. Consider this carefully.

If you are unable to make an arrangement to borrow

money from a family member or friend, your next best option may be a bank or credit union.

When borrowing from a financial institution it will generally involve you working face-to-face with a customer service representative at the organization. You will be asked to complete an application and determine how much money they will loan you and how you will repay this loan. You can view this as a good opportunity to improve your credit situation by paying this loan back according to the agreement.

If you have a bank account, the institution that has your account will be more likely to loan you money than somewhere that you are not already doing business.

If the representative is suggesting a re-payment plan that is not realistic for you, tell them. DO NOT make an agreement that you know you cannot fulfill. Let them know that you will not be able to meet those terms and the reasons why. They will generally propose another payment plan that will work for you.

Most of these approaches to solving your money problem will depend on your having maintained good credit.

There is an additional way in which you can borrow money but I never recommend this. These businesses are often called "Pay Day" loans or "Cash Advance" loans. Often they will loan $50-200. It is quick and easy to get money this way, often without any kind of background check. But the interest charged on your loan is usually very high.

The interest charged on pay day loans can be anywhere from $10 to $30 per $100 borrowed. The interest is much higher than the 8% we discussed above. The idea is that you will repay this loan with money from your next check.

Sometimes what happens though is that the borrowing becomes a vicious cycle. Let's say you did not have $200 to pay for an emergency expense. You borrow money to pay for the expense, but nothing has changed with your income, so the next pay day you actually owe $200 plus $30 in interest. You pay that off according to the agreement, but now you don't have that $230 in your budget to pay the other expenses now due. So you borrow again. Now you are borrowing $230 plus $33 interest. Now you owe $263.00 The interest keeps building so you get further and further in debt. How will you pay that?

There is also another concern. In some cases you are asked to give the lending business the title to your car to secure the amount of money you borrow. If you are unable to pay back the loan, the car becomes the lenders. Now, without a car, how will you get back and forth to work? So your paychecks stop. Then you aren't able to pay your other bills.

This makes a loan with a fixed rate of interest and regular payments that you can afford look much better. Can you see why I don't recommend this option? There is almost always another way to borrow money without the huge interest rates on "pay day" loans and the likelihood of continuing to have to borrow to meet recurring expenses.

Identity Theft

Just as there are bad drivers on the road who try to cut you off there are people who attempt to steal your identity, including your driver's license number, Social Security number, and good credit. Some identity thieves take the actual driver's license, Social Security card, or other documents that contain personal information.

Sometimes identifying information is stolen from one's mailbox through items delivered to your address or from outgoing checks placed in the mailbox for mail pickup.

Never leave identifying information in your mailbox.

In other cases people will hack into online records and obtain personal information. Either way, the result is the same. They can create misery for the person whose identity has been stolen. In many cases the thieves will use the stolen identity to open up charge accounts and purchase very expensive items. If you have your identity stolen and you do not discover it for a while it is possible that you will be responsible for paying for the items the thief has stolen.

Should you find that your identity has been stolen, immediately report it to your local police. This should prevent you from being liable for the items that the thief has stolen or debts the thief has created in your name. Also, immediately report the theft to one of the credit bureaus listed above. The credit bureau you contact will then contact the other two credit bureaus. Any company that subsequently checks on your credit to open an account for someone pretending to be you will be notified of the identity theft. This will keep the bad guys from making any more fraudulent charges.

If your identity has been stolen, you may be unable to open accounts or rent apartments as quickly as usual because your true identity will need to be verified.

The credit bureaus will give you the opportunity to put a free security alert on your account for ninety days while you attempt to work with locations where someone has falsely used your identity. By contacting the credit bureaus you will be allowed to check your credit report at no charge several times within the next year to be sure that there are no other fraudulent charges in your name.

There are services online that can help with identify theft protection. By goggling "identity theft protection" you may find a number of companies that provide protection for you. Possible services can be found at LifeLock.com and Experian.com.

Be sure to check for any associated fees for this service.

Document Security

You will generally need to have your driver's license or personal identity card with you at all times. You will likely have other important documents that you will need to keep in a safe place.

A fireproof box is recommended.

It is also a good idea to have copies of important documents in a separate location, such as your parent's home, the home of a trusted friend, or a safety deposit box that you rent from your bank.

Some people keep extra copies of their important documents in a "grab box." This is easily accessible and can be grabbed in the event of a fire or other disaster that would make it necessary to leave your residence in a hurry.

Some of the items you might want to keep in the grab box or other secure box are Social Security cards, bank account numbers, rental agreements or deeds to property, insurance papers, automobile titles, school records, etc. It is a good idea to keep copies of all of your wallet items and documents in your smart phone in a safe place as well, in case your wallet or phone is ever stolen.

If your wallet or phone containing your personal documents is stolen, it may require a great deal of time and money to replace these documents. Some of the documents may be replaceable but will likely have the same number on them that your thief now has.

It is possible to apply for a new Social Security number but you must be able to prove your card was stolen. Proving this may require obtaining a police report for which you will have to pay. You may also have to prove that someone is using your number or that they are harassing or abusing you.

It will be helpful to designate a permanent location to file all important papers. Some people use metal file cabinets, others use cardboard boxes. It is recommended that important papers be stored in some type of fire proof container, in case of fire. These can be purchased at office supply stores.

It is a good idea to keep duplicate copies of the items stored in your grab box. This will allow you easy access to those items, if needed, without disturbing the grab box.

It is helpful to alphabetize the file folders in which you store your documents. Some of the folders might include:

- Auto registration
- Auto repairs
- Auto insurance
- Auto title
- Bank accounts
- Birth certificates
- Credit card information
- Employment applications and contracts
- Family documents
- Health insurance
- Lease agreements
- Letters of recommendation
- Life insurance
- Medical records
- Passport
- Pet papers (immunizations and registrations)
- Routine bills
- School papers
- Utilities
- Voter registration card

You might choose to group several of these items together, for instance, you could put all auto-related information in one folder. As you work on your filing system, you will find a way to file that makes the most sense to you. It doesn't matter exactly how these folders are labeled, as long as the system works for you.

Some people choose to put much of this information on their computers. If this works best for you remember to use passwords that no one can figure out based on other identifying information.

It is a good idea to change your password every 3- 6 months to prevent others from figuring it out and gaining access to your personal information.

There will also be some documents that you must keep hard copies of, so having an organized place to keep these will be very helpful.

Frequently back up all of the information stored on your computer in case your computer crashes!

Resources

https://www.mint.com
https://www.personalcapital.com
https://www.tiller.com
https://quickbooks.intuit.com
https://venmo.com
https://paypal.com/us/home
https://www.acorn.com
https://www.stash.com
https://lifelock.com
www.experian.com

2

Resume Writing

It is never too late to be what you might have been.

— George Elliot

Resume writing can be a daunting task, but a necessary one when searching for a job. Your resume is a chance for you to look in your rearview mirror and share with a potential employer the roads that have gotten you to this point in your life's journey. This is your opportunity to toot your own horn and describe the strengths and past experiences that make you a good employee. You are entering the professional world. Your resume should appear professional as well.

Preparing to Write a Professional Resume

Some people find it hard to talk (or write) about themselves. As you are developing your resume it is important to ask yourself several questions:

1. Why do I want this job?

2. What do I know about this organization and job opening?

3. What is this organization looking for? Generally, employers look for positive attitudes, loyalty, good relationship skills, someone who will treat their customers with respect.

4. What is my best asset?

5. What personality traits do I have that will be appropriate for this position? These describe who you are. Am I friendly and outgoing, trustworthy, adaptable? Do I interact well with others?

6. What professional skills do I have? These describe what I can do. Am I trained in CPR? Am I able to set up spread sheets or do Power Point presentations? Usually these are things someone has been taught or has learned to do.

7. Employers are also looking for people with strong "soft skills". These might include teamwork, leadership, critical thinking, problem-solving, etc.

Traits are subjective and are difficult to measure. Skills are objective and easily measured. Soft skills, however, are a little more difficult to measure.

8. Which type of resume format do I want to follow? (See choices below.)

Your resume will contain different information than anyone else's does based on your experiences and education, and will therefore look different from others.

Resumes should always be typed. If you do not have access to a computer have a family member, teacher, or friend help you type your resume. This may be the first look an employer has at you. You want to sell yourself.

Spend a few extra dollars to purchase high-quality paper to help your resume stand out from others.

Always store your resume on a computer *and* a flash drive. You will constantly be changing your resume to suit particular job opportunities. It is much easier to change things or move information around if it is stored on your computer.

Most resumes, no matter which type, contain the following information:

- Full name (no nicknames)
- Complete physical address
- Phone numbers

- Email address
- Objective (i.e., seeking a job in marketing)
- Prior work experience
- Educational background, including any supervised practicums or internships you completed
- Volunteer / Service Learning or Community experiences
- Awards or recognition of excellence
- References

You may wish to include other headings such as "Certificates Earned" if it is relevant to the job for which you are applying.

Be sure you include first and last names of supervisors and other references

Pictures are almost never included in resumes.

Specify which phone number is your cell number and which number is your home phone if you are listing both.

Be sure that the voice messages on your phones are very professional. Your friends may want to hear that "Hot Mama" or "The Dude" wants them to leave a message after hearing your favorite tune, but most employers would prefer to hear mature, professional messages. Think about the types of people with whom you have interviewed and at least temporarily change your messages to something that may be more appealing to them.

Whenever you are answering or returning phone calls pay attention to any background noise around you. Be sure the television is off and no one is talking or yelling in the background.

Format

Most employers are very busy people. It is important to create a resume that is easy to read and not too wordy. A resume that is broken up by headings is easier to read and allows potential employers to quickly reference the areas in which they are most interested.

Begin by placing your name, address, and contact information at the top of the page, generally in the center of the page. Your name, address, phone number, and email address should each be on a separate line, in that order.

Next, you will put a heading of either "Employment," "Experience," or "Education" based on the type of resume you wish to develop. You will need to decide if you want to put these headings in italics, bold, or bold italics, and what font size you want to use. Whatever you decide, all headings must be in the same format.

Usually, the heading is placed on the left side of the page. The dates or skills (depending on which type of resume you choose) can be listed below the heading, and the information detailing each item should be indented so that your resume is easy to read.

Leave plenty of white space on your resume and make it no longer than two pages. If you are able, present yourself on a single page.

The font size of the body text (everything under the headings) should be 12 so that your resume is easy to read.

Resumes should be as concise as possible.

There are many, many sample resumes online. By googling "resumes" online you will find many different sample resumes. Below are summaries of the standard resumes.

Do not put on a resume that you left a job because your boss would not let you have time off to go to dinner with your family. This may tell the potential employer that you do not put a priority on your job or their business.

Types of Resumes

There are three common types of resumes: chronological, functional, and mixed. A chronological resume lists experiences and education in the order they occurred. A functional resume emphasizes the kinds of experiences you have had. A mixed resume is a combination of the chronological and functional.

Chronological Resume

A chronological resume will focus on a *history* of your experiences and education, listing the most recent employment you held or school you attended, with dates. If you have a section for employment, this section should include the dates of employment (January, 2007–present), the title of your position (sales clerk), and a brief description of your responsibilities in this position (responsible for customer service, scheduling of employees, stocking, etc.). If you left a place of employment for acceptable reasons you will want to include why you left (better hours, higher pay, moved to a new city, etc.). If you left because you and your boss had a fight or you did not follow rules, do not state that on your resume.

When listing educational experiences include the name of the school, the dates you attended, and your field of study. If you received a degree or certificate from an educational institution be sure to include that information as well.

Functional Resume

A functional resume will show an employer the skills that you have demonstrated in the past, such as officer of a club at school, positions held in scouting or other organizations, experience in fundraising efforts, etc. List the type of skill (sales, management, etc.) followed by a description of how you demonstrated that skill. If you choose, include the length of time or dates during which you performed these skills. Below, give your educational credentials.

Stop All employers will want to know your level of education. Most jobs require a minimal educational level. The employer will often check this information first as it will not be necessary to interview you if you do not have the minimum requirements for a certain position.

Mixed Resume

Some resumes mix work and educational experiences together. You are attempting to show an employer what you have done, so it is fine to combine these two categories. If you choose to do this you can list everything under a general heading of "Experience."

Other resumes have two headings, "Work Experience" and "Education," and list previous jobs and educational experience in chronological order. (These two headings may be reversed, showing "Education" first, if that is more relevant to the job for which you are applying.)

Caution Most resumes include a heading for volunteer experience, service learning or community service, under which you list any organizations for which you volunteered and the duties you completed. Employers like to know that employees are unselfish enough to give some of their time freely to help others.

Content

Everyone has to start somewhere. If you are applying for your first job, emphasize your strengths and interests in your resume. Show the employer that you are anxious to work and do a good job for the company.

Sometimes it seems that experience in a previous job or volunteer experience will not be relevant to the job for which you are presently applying, but employers often see it differently. Let's say you are applying for a position to do intakes at a social service agency. Past work as a McDonald's cashier will show that you are able to greet the public and communicate well with clients. This could end up landing you the job. Resume Genius is a great help with resume content and questions you may have about what to include in your resume.

Introductory or Cover Letter

It is a good idea to include an introductory letter with your resume. This would be the first item the potential employer will see. A good cover letter may determine whether or not you receive an opportunity to interview.

This should be a one page letter addressed to the person identified on the job posting. It is best to attempt to obtain the name and correct spelling of the person who will be reviewing your resume. If that is not possible, it is appropriate to address it "To Whom it May Concern" or "Dear Sir or Ma'am".

The purpose of the letter is to introduce yourself and explain why you are a good candidate for the position that is available. This is when you get a chance to include some positive things about yourself that may not have fit well into your resume. Resume Genius, mentioned above, also discusses roadblocks to your work history and how to handle these in your cover letter.

Presentation

Carefully review your finished product. Try to look at your resume as a potential employer might. Check for the following:

1. Be sure it is typed. Carefully review for any typos or misspelling. It can be helpful to read your resume out loud to yourself or to others. By doing this you will sometimes catch mistakes that you over looked.

2. Have you used a good quality paper?

3. Are there any stains on the resume?

4. Are all of the headings in the same location and using the same font and style as each other?

5. Did you use correct grammar and not slang?

6. If you are currently employed, did you talk about that job in the present tense, not the past tense as should be used in previous job descriptions?

 For fun, once you complete your resume, you

might take a photo of yourself and lay it on top of your resume. Does your photo match who you portrayed in the resume? Is it time for a haircut or better choices of clothing before you present your resume to any one?

If you are presenting your resume in person, place it in a professional-looking folder or envelope. Type or neatly write the name of the recipient on the envelope.

Check to make sure there are no coffee stains or dirty fingerprints on either your cover letter, resume, or the envelope.

You are now prepared to begin your job search.

Resources

https://resumegenius.com/cover-letters-the-how-to-guide.
https://www.indeed.com

3

Searching for a Job

> *The only person you are destined to become*
> *is the person you decide to be.*
>
> — Ralph Waldo Emerson

There are several benefits to obtaining a job as a young person. A job is the first opportunity a teen has to prove that he or she is a responsible and motivated hard worker. This also shows a teen that he or she can successfully achieve a goal. A very motivated teen might be able to save enough money for a down payment on a car or another item of value. Many teens choose to start a savings account for college or another major purchase.

Locating Places to Interview

Some people are interested in earning money at a young age and will often hold their first jobs when they are fourteen or fifteen. These are generally one-time or short-term jobs that either the adolescent or his or her parents arrange. Common examples include mowing yards, babysitting, or cleaning houses and garages.

Once a teen reaches the age of sixteen, he or she is able to apply for jobs that pay by the hour, week, or month. There are several ways to find a job.

Most jobs are located through networking. A person's network consists of family, relatives, friends, or acquaintances from church, school, Scouts, or other activities. Contact these folks to see if they are aware of job openings. Talk to as many people as you can, let them know you are interested in working, and tell them what type of job you hope to obtain.

People talk! So put your best foot forward and don't hesitate to let them ask their friends and contacts about possible job openings for you as well.

Many people turn to the internet to search for jobs. Often job openings are posted online based on your job preference and/or location. If you are looking for a specific job (or not sure what you want to do) you might begin your search by exploring different job titles. By "googling" lawyer, stone mason, mechanic, or any other job title, you are likely to find a description of the job, tasks and responsibilities, average annual income, availability of jobs, etc. Maybe you have heard of social workers, but don't have any idea what a social worker does. This is a good way to identify jobs you are interested in or want to become trained to do. Some very helpful sites are usajobs.gov, todaysmilitary.com, and Craigslist.org.

Students in middle school are now being asked to choose a career pathway. Among the choices of careers are health services, education, social services, or science areas. Having a summer job or interning at an organization is a way to explore different types of jobs.

Some people prefer to look in the classified section of their local newspaper. Jobs in the newspaper generally are located under the title of the job, such as welder or secretary. Many communities also have local newspapers available at convenience stores and other businesses. These are free and list a number of different job opportunities.

Many schools and public places will post job openings on bulletin boards. Colleges usually have job placement centers where employers post vacancies they would like to fill.

Colleges generally will offer various assessment tools that will help you identify your skills and areas of interests. They will also help people develop job skills and write resumes.

Some people decide to go from business to business inquiring about possible job openings.

If you choose to physically go to various locations to pick up applications, go inside the office. *Do not* go to the drive-through window as that will make you appear lazy.

Be sure to shake hands with those you meet at the organization. If you are meeting a woman, let her reach out her hand to shake first. If she does not initiate shaking hands, then make eye contact, smile and give a slight nod.

If you choose to search for a job or pick up applications in person, it is imperative that you are clean and well dressed: slacks and a nice shirt for men, and slacks and a nice blouse for women (see Chapter 4, Keeping Your Job). Flip flops and zip up hoodies are not appropriate. Demonstrate a friendly attitude and a pleasant smile.

If you are seeking a job at a fast food restaurant or other eating establishment, don't go at meal times as this is when they are the busiest. The manager will probably not be available to see you then and will ask you to come back at a different time.

Often, the very first person with whom you speak, whether it is a secretary or another employee, may be asked by his or her employer about how you looked and how you presented yourself when you spoke with them. Employers want to know if you were respectful, polite, well spoken, and neatly dressed. First impressions are critical.

Note how the employees you see are dressed. This will give you some idea of how you should dress if you are asked to return for an interview.

Completing Job Applications

If there is a job opening or the employer is potentially interested in hiring you, he or she might ask you to complete an application immediately. The application could be printed out or available online. Some businesses will give you an application to take home and complete.

Ask the employer if he or she prefers that the application be returned in person or by email or mail.

If the employer would like you to take the application home to complete and return the application by mail, be sure you obtain the correct name and spelling of the person who will receive the application and their proper title (Dr., Mr., etc.). Be sure you have the correct mailing address. He or she may want you to mail your application to a post office box instead of to the physical address of the business.

Applications typically require personal information such as name, address, phone, and email address. You will be asked about any past job experiences, how long you were at each job, and the reasons for leaving. Applications will request the name, address, and phone numbers of people the employer can contact as references.

Sometimes the application will specify that the references include personal references or credit references.

Do not give the name of a relative as a personal reference. Employers tend to think that relatives are very biased and will not give an objective reference. The reference of a relative could be extra great or extra bad!

Contact those people you plan to use as references in advance and ask their permission to list him or her as a reference. It is important to give your references' correct titles (Dr., Mr., etc.), include their first and last names, spell their names correctly, and make sure their contact information is accurate. Check with the references as to whether they would like to be contacted during the day or evening, and if they prefer for you to give potential employers their work, home, or cell phone numbers.

All of your application information should be stored in a folder that you carry with you when you are job searching. If you are asked to complete an application immediately, you will have all of the necessary information with you.

CAUTION

If you are able to take the application home with you, make a copy of it before you fill it out. That way you can use the copy as a rough draft in case you make a mistake.

CAUTION

Use a pencil when filling out the rough draft. If you realize that you need to revise the information you have given, you can erase it on the rough draft.

Complete the application neatly, using a black pen. Use a dictionary to check the spelling of any words of which you are uncertain.

Attach a resume to your job applications. This will give the employer information about your accomplishments and work experience. (See Chapter 2, Resume Writing, for information on how to develop a resume.)

CAUTION

Have several copies of your resume in your folder in case you are asked to provide one.

Some employers ask for additional information such as credit history. Your credit history will tell them how you have managed your finances and will reflect your level of responsibility.

Employers are also likely to search Facebook, Twitter, Instagram, and other social networks to attempt to learn more about you. Some people place inappropriate pictures of themselves online, or their friends place them there. Many employers regularly check these sites. If employers see inappropriate photos or comments on any social media sights, it may reflect poorly on you.

Always be aware when you are in public that most cell phones have the capability of taking photographs, and that there might be security cameras in place. Don't do anything that might later embarrass you or even keep you from getting a job.

Many employers also want to know if you have ever been charged with or convicted of any crimes. If you have, they will want to know if the crime was a misdemeanor or a felony. If you have any kind of criminal background, be prepared to explain the charges or convictions as well as any punishment you received.

Some very large companies will hire felons, so don't be discouraged about applying for jobs if you have a criminal background.

Once you have completed an application, make a copy of it to keep in your file at home. This will save you a lot of time the next time you complete a job application, as the next application you complete will probably request much of the same information.

Now that you have completed the job application, you will return it to the potential employer either by mail or in person.

Enclose a cover letter with the application. This letter should be dated and addressed to the employer, and it should briefly thank the employer for taking the time to review your application. (See Introductory Cover Letter in Chapter 2, Resume Writing). You might also tell him or her that you are looking forward to hearing from him or her soon. By including a cover letter you are not only showing respect to the employer but also helping your application stand out from all of the others.

If you do not get a response within two weeks of turning in an application, it is appropriate to contact the company. Let the employer know that you do not want to bother them or take too much of their time but that you want to ask if they have had an opportunity to review your application. You can also let them know that you hope he/she will be interested in interviewing you.

Speak slowly and clearly when speaking to others, and thank them for their time.

Once the company has reviewed your application they will decide if they would like to interview you. If so, they will contact you and set an appointment for an interview.

Preparing for an Interview

To get a job you will probably need to have an interview with someone in the Human Resources department or the manager or owner of the company. Once you make an appointment for an interview, it will be even more important to obtain any additional information you can about the prospective employer. Talk to people who have worked there or have experience with the company. You might also contact the city information bureau to learn about how the company contributes to the community.

Be sure to search online for the company's website. It is important for you to learn as much as you can about the job and the organization. Try to find out exactly what the purpose of the business is, their mission statement, the kinds of people they serve, the types of services they provide, and their history. Researching the company on the Internet may be very productive. You can often be successful in gathering information by going to www.google.com and typing in the name of the business or the category of business.

By learning about the business in advance you may find there are questions you would like to ask during the interview. Employers will be impressed to know that you have spent time learning about their organization and are not applying for a job just to get a paycheck.

There are some questions that employers typically ask during job interviews.

Reviewing the sample questions and thinking through some responses should help tremendously with your answers in the actual interview.

Review your social media sites and remove anything questionable or inappropriate. That way if a potential interviewer should check those sites, they will not find anything inappropriate.

The interviewer might possibly ask why you would like to work for their organization. He or she will probably also ask what you see as your strengths and weaknesses, expecting you to identify some weaknesses. (Everyone has some weaknesses, and being able to acknowledge these shows self-awareness on your part.) You might add that the weaknesses you named might include things you would like to improve by working at this business.

Interviewers will often ask open-ended questions—ones that require more than a "yes" or "no" answer. Take a minute to think about your answers to their questions before responding. You do not want to appear nervous or confused.

Dressing for an Interview

First impressions are extremely important. The way you dress sends messages. Be sure you are sending the messages you want others to receive. For job interviews, you want to look your most professional. Hygiene, general appearance, and facial expressions are the first things people notice. Shower, use deodorant, and brush your teeth prior to your interview. If you are a smoker, be sure your attire is free from the smell of smoke.

When considering your attire for an interview, maintain a professional look, not a "party" or "after-five" look.

Clothes should be clean and pressed. For a company with a more formal atmosphere, males should wear a suit or sports coat. In other cases, it may be appropriate for men to wear a nice shirt and slacks. Typically, women should wear a dress or suit and heels. In some organizations, it is appropriate for women to wear a nice blouse, slacks and shoes.

Many employers will look at your footwear to see if your shoes are clean and polished. Wearing open-toed sandals or flip-flops is not appropriate for a job interview. You can always dress down once you have landed the job, if the position requires that, but it is best to dress nicely for an interview.

If you have been inside this establishment before, think about the way the employees were dressed. This will give you some ideas on the appropriate dress for this organization.

People have a wide variety of attitudes regarding tattoos and piercings. In your job interview, you are hoping to impress the employer and land the job. Because you do not know the attitude or age of the person interviewing you, cover any tattoos and remove any facial piercings. A single pair of earrings for women is considered appropriate. Earrings should not be extravagant. You may find more tips about grooming in Chapter 4, Keeping Your Job.

If it is essential to you that your tattoos and nontraditional piercings be visible, you should ask about the company's policy regarding tattoos and piercings *during* the interview. If you do not agree with their policy, you should explain your position. If you feel very strongly about it and the company does not agree with you, you may decide that you do not want to work at this organization.

CAUTION

If your convictions about tattoos and piercings are very strong, keep in mind that this will reduce the number of potential employers.

If you find you and the interviewer have different opinions on tattoos and piercings and that this is a roadblock to you working at his/her organization, thank him or her for their time, as you do not want to appear rude or unappreciative of them taking the time to interview you. Let the person know that you feel very strongly about this issue and therefore will be unable to work there.

If it is not essential that you be able to expose your tattoos and piercings, wait until after you land the job to ask about the company's policy regarding tattoos and piercings, and be prepared to abide by the policy.

An Actual Interview

The person who interviews you will take the lead. He or she will ask you questions about your work experience, interests, hours you are available to work, and possibly why you would like to work for this organization. He or she will probably also ask what you see as your strengths and weaknesses, expecting you to identify some weaknesses. (Everyone has some weaknesses, and being able to acknowledge these shows self-awareness on your part.) The weaknesses you name might include things you would like to improve by working at this business.

Interviewers will often ask open-ended questions— ones that require more than a yes or no answer. Take a minute to think about your answers to their questions before responding. You do not want to appear nervous or confused.

Some of the questions that interviewers might ask are listed below.

1. Tell me something about yourself.

2. How would you describe yourself?

3. How would a friend or teacher describe you?

4. What inspires you to put forth your greatest effort?

5. Why should I hire you?

6. How do you determine or evaluate success?

7. What two accomplishments have given you the most satisfaction and why?

8. In what kind of work environment are you most comfortable?

Reviewing the sample questions and thinking through some responses should help tremendously with your answers.

When responding to the interviewer's questions it is always good to answer with "Yes" or "No." Never respond with "Yeah," "Um," "Huh," or "Like." Speak very clearly and slowly so that the interviewer does not have to ask you to repeat your answers.

The interviewer may ask if you have any questions. This is a good time to clarify any information you have obtained about the company prior to the interview. You can also ask about appropriate dress, hours of work, job expectations and responsibilities, etc.

Writing down your questions and taking them with you to the interview can help you remember everything you wish to ask an interviewer.

It is best to let the employer bring up discussions of salary. He or she may make you an offer or ask what you are expecting to be paid. The websites mentioned in Chapter 3, Searching for a Job, may help you determine what a reasonable salary is for various positions in your location. If you have no idea what a reasonable salary is, you might say that you are unsure of what the current salary is for a position like this, or you might suggest a pay range that you consider fair.

Once you have completed the interview, thank the interviewer for his or her time. He or she will generally tell you when they will contact you. If not, then ask when you might expect to hear from them.

They are usually very busy people, so do not be too pushy.

Always send a thank you note to the people who interviewed you. Let them know that you enjoyed meeting them, and thank them again for their time. Tell them that you look forward to hearing from them. (This might also encourage them to review your application a little more quickly if they have not already reviewed it.)

The thank you note should be an actual card or note, not an email message. You want to appear as professional as possible.

Documenting Interviews

Keep a list of agencies where you interviewed, the interviewers' names, dates to expect to hear from the various businesses, and dates when you should contact them. Also note things you have observed or discussed during the interview—that they have kids, like chocolate, are interested in fishing, or any other personal information you can recall.

The organization should contact you whether or not they offer you a job. When they do, be sure to thank them for calling you back. If they offer you a job, they will probably discuss pay, hours of work, and the date you can begin employment. This is another important time to thank them and tell them how much you appreciate the job. Add that you are looking forward to working for them and that you hope they will be pleased with your performance.

If the company does not hire you, keep in mind that they may offer you a position at some point in the future. You may not have gotten the job this time because other applicants were more mature, more experienced, had their applications in sooner, or could work different hours. Thank them for contacting you and taking the time to consider you. If you are still interested, ask them to keep your application on file for future openings in their organization.

If you feel comfortable doing so, ask them if they have any suggestions regarding changes you might make when interviewing for future jobs.

If this company did not offer you a job, ask if they can refer you to another employer.

Most people interview for many jobs before actually receiving an offer. Even though it is very disappointing when you are rejected for a job, remember that it is not the only job in the world. Use this as an opportunity to improve your job-searching skills.

Review in your mind everything that happened during the interviewing process, including questions about your application or resume. Also ask yourself, "Did I dress appropriately, ask important questions, look interested in obtaining the job, have information about the workplace, and share the skills I have?" Decide if there is anything you would like to do differently on your next job interview.

Make notes of any ideas you have for future interviewing and place them in your folder with your other interviewing information.

Keep your chin up, and talk to yourself about how important you are and how the next job opening might be the perfect one for you. Remember that interviewing for a job can be a full-time job in itself. It is a process, not a one-time event.

Resources

https://www.usajobs.gov
todaysmilitary.com
https://www.craigslist.org

4

Keeping Your Job

*The only place success comes before work
is in the dictionary.*

— Vince Lombardi

If you have been hired to fill an available position, your employer must feel that you will be a good employee. Many employers look for people who have good attitudes rather than specific job skills. They feel they can teach employees whatever skills are necessary, but believe it is very difficult to change someone's attitude. So, present your best attitude.

Professional Behaviors

Below are some of the things employers expect employees to do if the employees intend to keep their job.

Be on Time

Employees are expected to report to work on time. It is best to arrive five to ten minutes early so that you have a few minutes to put your personal things away and begin thinking about your responsibilities for the day.

If you are relieving someone from a shift that they are completing, it is important to report a few minutes early so that the person on the previous shift is able to leave when their shift is over and they will not have to stay late to wait for you to appear on the job.

There may be times when situations occur that prevent you from arriving on time. Perhaps there is a traffic jam on the way to work, or you have a flat tire. In that case, immediately call your employer and explain the reason for your absence or tardiness. People are generally understanding about unusual situations if you communicate with them about your situation. If they do not hear from you, however, they may become frustrated and be less patient and understanding.

When you call in late, let your employer know the approximate time you expect to report for work.

Maintain Good Hygiene

Hygiene is an issue that affects all of your relationships, including those at work. Some of the following guidelines will seem obvious, but many people lose their jobs because they ignore them.

1. Bathe every day.

     Use soap!

2. Wash your hair at least every other day.

    Clean hair is great, but it needs to be brushed as well.

3. Brush your teeth two to three times a day and use mouthwash. Keep breath mints in your pocket if you are unable to brush your teeth after lunch.

    If you are a smoker, always brush your teeth or at least use breath mints after smoking and before interacting with others.

    Try not to smoke in enclosed areas like your car. Smoke is absorbed in clothing. You may be around someone with asthma or other breathing problems. Exposure to smoke may put their health at risk.

Dress Appropriately

Now that you are traveling into the world of work it

is important to give some thought as to how you will dress. You want to appear professional and classy, not cheap or shabby, even if you are dressing casually. Clothing should enhance your appearance and not be suggestive or distracting. You constantly send messages about who you are through the way you choose to dress.

Depending on your place of employment, appropriate clothing for a man may be anything from a suit and tie to nice jeans and a collared shirt. Women may be expected to wear a dress or skirt and heels or jeans and a collared shirt or blouse. Some organizations may not require collared shirts or tops.

Below are some tips to help you with appropriate grooming and dress.

1. Clothing should not be too short, too low cut, or too tight.

2. Tops should not reveal an excessive amount of skin. Clothing that allows underwear to be visible is not acceptable.

3. "Hip-huggers" or low-cut pants, jeans, or shorts must be worn with tops that are tucked in or are long enough to cover any skin when your arms are raised.

4. Body piercings should be removed and tattoos covered at work. Dangling earrings and excessive jewelry are also not recommended.

5. T-shirts may or may not be appropriate in your work environment.

    If you are allowed to wear T-shirts on the job, most employers will require that any writing on the shirts be tasteful: no foul language, no messages about alcohol or drugs, or offensive material.

6. Some organizations will require that you wear closed-toed shoes for safety. Flip- flops are not considered professional dress.

7. Practice good hygiene, taking baths, brushing teeth, and using mouthwash and deodorant.

8. Torn and stained garments are not acceptable. Garments should be clean and ironed.

9. Sagging pants are not acceptable.

    Appropriate clothing does not have to be expensive. If you need to purchase clothes that are appropriate work attire, and money is an issue, try thrift stores and consignment stores. They often sell nice items for very reasonable prices.

    Always check your appearance, front and back, in a full-length mirror before leaving the house.

Interpersonal Relationships

Maintaining healthy relationships with supervisors and coworkers is very important to success on the job.

To establish and maintain good work relationships it is important to begin with a positive, friendly attitude.

When meeting people, look them in the eye, smile, repeat their name (people like to hear their own name and it helps you remember it), and give them a firm handshake.

People appreciate being called by name. Continue to do so each time you see them.

Some people may be threatened by your presence. Get to know them and assure them that you are not there to take their jobs. You might tell them a little about yourself or ask for their suggestions or input.

Some people feel more secure in their jobs if you ask them questions or ask for assistance.

Be sure to greet fellow workers and supervisors each day, but do not waste time talking excessively.

As you are learning about your new job, be sure to clarify expectations. Now is a good time to ask about work hours, appropriate dress, to whom you report, where you sign in, and any other questions you may have about your employer's expectations.

If you are unclear about instructions or expectations ask for clarification. Employers would rather

have you ask questions than complete a task inappro-
priately and waste valuable time doing it over.

Most businesses will have some type of orientation or
policy manual. Become familiar with all of the policies
so that you can follow the company rules.

If you don't understand the reason behind a policy, ask about it. Sometimes getting clarification can
help you do your job more efficiently. Other times, the
policy is based on reasons that have become obsolete,
and asking about it makes the employers realize they
should update it.

Treating your supervisor, coworkers, and customers with respect will gain you respect as well. Saying
"Please" and "Thank you" is always appreciated.

All people have personal problems of some sort. It is
imperative that you leave yours at home. The workplace is not where you should make personal phone
calls or set appointments unrelated to work. These
things should be done on your own time.

At almost every place of employment some employees
will participate in what is known as the rumor mill.
This is where all of the gossip is shared. Listening to
and sharing gossip can be very dangerous, as the information is often inaccurate and sometimes hurtful.

Do not participate in the rumor mill.

If someone tries to include you in the rumor mill, kindly say "I am not interested in hearing or spreading rumors. Let's talk about something else."

People will soon learn that you are not willing to participate in gossip and that they can trust you not to spread information.

Office Etiquette

How you handle yourself in the office can be critical to earning a raise or promotion. Demonstrating courtesy and a positive attitude are keys to being successful. There are some suggestions below you may find helpful.

1. When in the office, if you need to speak with someone, approach their office door and check to see if they are on the phone or have someone in their office. If not, ask if they have time to talk with you. If they are busy, step away from the door and wait patiently for them to be able to see you.

2. Don't talk rudely and sarcastically. Be sure you are using respectful language.

3. Turn off your cell phone and put it with your other personal possessions. You are not being paid to

talk on the phone, check your personal messages, or text your friends.

4. Cell phone conversations should not occur in the restroom. This is a time and place for privacy. Others do not appreciate listening to bathroom sounds during their cell phone calls.

5. Be considerate of other people's suggestions, opinions, and feelings.

6. Do not eat food that other people have put in the refrigerator.

Communication

Communication is a key to successful relationships with coworkers, bosses, and customers. Learning to be polite and communicate in a positive manner is essential to your success.

Here are some very basic steps to communication and relationship building that will help you be successful at your job.

1. Smile

2. Speak clearly

3. Do not use curse words—cursing is considered rude and disrespectful. People usually curse when they do not know how to speak appropriately or they choose not to express themselves in an appropriate way. Replacing curse words with appro-

priate language will help you travel your route to success more smoothly.

4. Remember to call people by name. Addressing people by name is always appreciated. In some parts of the country, using the terms "ma'am" and "sir" is appreciated as well. Being respectful of others is one way to show your integrity.

5. Say what you mean.

6. Treat others as you would like to be treated.

7. Try to solve problems instead of complaining about things.

8. Be part of the solution, not part of the problem.

9. Clean up after yourself.

10. Be considerate of others.

11. Offer to help coworkers when they are having trouble with a task or need to take a break.

12. Be a team player. Workers who are uncooperative will not get raises or be promoted.

13. Be on time and ready to start work.

14. Better yet, arrive five minutes early.

15. Volunteer to do extra work.

Strengths and Weaknesses

People bring to their jobs and relationships all of the experiences, issues, and frustrations that have made them who they are today. Part of what they bring will be strengths and part will be weaknesses. Some strengths people may have might include a positive attitude, a healthy self-esteem, an ability to listen well, and the desire to be a team player.

Try to identify your own strengths and weaknesses so that you can emphasize your positive characteristics on the job.

Some people consider their weaknesses as baggage. This baggage can interfere with their ability to form positive, healthy relationships at work. It might result in them feeling jealousy, frustration, insecurity, hostility, and low self-esteem.

Other people's baggage can interfere with what you or they might be trying to accomplish. Perhaps you remind them of a parent or friend with whom they have a bad relationship so it is difficult for them to relate to you in a positive way.

Emphasize strengths at work. Recognize that weaknesses often are strengths taken to an extreme. Evaluate your weaknesses and modify your behavior accordingly.

Dealing with Conflict

Should your supervisors or coworkers bring their baggage to work, their interpersonal relationships may be impacted by their attitudes, feelings, and behaviors.

Perhaps they have had a fight with a significant other before reporting for work. They might take their anger or frustration out on you.

Ask yourself, "Are they having a bad day, or did I behave in a way that warranted their reaction?"

In some cases, when a coworker appears angry or upset, the best choice is to withdraw. Leave the room, if necessary, or ask if this situation can be discussed after a time-out.

Sometimes people make comments out of their own frustration and it has nothing to do with you. Don't take it personally.

If you feel their behavior was uncalled for, it is appropriate to say something like, "It appears you are having a bad day. Is there something I can do to help you?"

If it is necessary to confront someone, try the Oreo method. The Oreo method has three parts. Part 1 is when you say something complimentary to or about the person or situation. Part 2 is when you express your concern and Part 3 is when you state something else positive.

An example of the Oreo method might be: "I am really glad you are at work today. When you are absent it slows down our work production and frustrates me.

I am so glad that we should be able to meet our quota today."

Using the Oreo method allows you to communicate with your coworkers in an unemotional way. It forces you to think about them positively and identify their strengths.

When you say something complimentary, then talk about the concern or criticism, and then say something else positive, you have sandwiched your criticism or concern, like the filling of an Oreo cookie, between the two outside layers of positive comments.

If you feel in some way responsible for a coworker's attitude toward you it is appropriate to discuss this. If an apology or explanation is called for, the professional thing to do is to make an apology or give an explanation.

An unemotional way to communicate an explanation, compliment or concern is by using an "I"-message. An "I"-message contains 3 parts. The parts include the feelings the speaker has, the situation or behavior that causes those feelings and why the situation or behavior makes you feel that way.

So an "I"-message looks like this:

I *feel* _____ *when* _____ *because* _____.

The "feeling" word needs to be an actual feeling, for example, sad, happy, proud, or frustrated. This can be used to explain a good or bad feeling. If you say, "I feel happy....." you are using a feeling word. If you say, "I feel like decking you.....", that is not describing a feeling.

So, a correct "I"-message might be, "*I feel happy when your grades are good because I know how hard you studied.*"

If you are upset about something and want to use an "I"-message you might say, "*I feel frustrated when you are running late and don't call because I worked hard to have dinner ready on time.*

This is so much better than saying, "Where in the heck have you been. You could have at least called. Dinner is cold now." If you say this it makes the other person feel defensive and likely an argument will begin.

CAUTION   An "I"-message may not work immediately or the first time. It is likely after several of these messages are used, that you will more likely be in a conversation rather than a fight.

Sometimes people don't know how to perceive someone else. Ask yourself or a friend or relative how they perceive you. Do they see you as friendly, cold, unhappy, pleasant?

See more information about communication in Chapter 13, Developing Interpersonal Communication and Problem Solving Skills

To begin relationships, share some of your own experiences.

Find something positive to say, or talk about something you have in common.

If you are unable to solve a situation through any of the above approaches, always follow the chain of command. That means that if you have tried to work out your problem with the person involved and have been unsuccessful, the next step would be discussing this issue with your supervisor (even if he or she is the problem).

Do not go over your supervisor's head to their supervisor unless you have already discussed the situation with your supervisor, and nothing has been done within a reasonable length of time.

Give your supervisor a chance to handle a situation before going over his or her head. No one appreciates being complained about without having had a chance to deal with the situation first.

On any job it is important that everyone be treated with respect and fairness. No business should tolerate harassment of any type. If you observe harassment or are a victim of harassment, date and document everything said and done in writing and make a copy of all documentation to keep at home. Harassment should be reported immediately to your supervisor in writing. If there is no response to your complaint of harassment, it is very appropriate to then go to the next person in charge.

Some businesses will have a human resources department, board of directors or licensing agency to which you can report harassment, particularly if the person harassing you holds a higher-ranking position than you hold.

See more about harassment in Chapter 12, Handling Social Issues and Relationships.

5

Finding Your Own Place to Live

It's nice finding that place where you can just go and relax.
— Moises Arias

Now that you have a source of income, whether you have landed a job or are receiving assistance from parents or some other source, it is time to find your own place to live. Having established a budget (Chapter 1, Managing Finances), you know how much money you will be able to pay each month for rent. You will also need to be sure you have enough money for the deposits on your residence and utilities. Most rental managers require a one-year lease, meaning that you agree to pay the rent each month for one year *whether you continue to live there or not.* There are several decisions to make before committing to a lease.

Decisions to Make

In what area of town would you like to live? Do you want it to be close to school, work, family, or friends? Do you want to live by yourself or with roommates? How many roommates would you like? Can you afford to pay utilities, or do the utility bills need to be included with your rent and paid by your landlord? Is the area safe? Is it close to a bus line if you do not have other transportation? Is it close to a grocery store? Do you want to rent an apartment, duplex or house? Is the residence furnished or unfurnished?

Finding a Place to Live

Once you have answered the above questions you are ready to find a place to live. There are several sources that can help you. Online resources include Zillow.com, Tulia.com and Craigslist.org. These online sites, among others, offer pictures of available rentals. They will also include all of the pertinent information regarding the properties that are available. They may also include times during which you can tour the properties.

The newspaper will list rentals in a section of the classifieds. Most papers divide the listings by apartments, duplexes, and houses. This should make your search easier. Each of the ads usually includes the following information

- Number of bedrooms
- Number of bathrooms

- Whether or not appliances are provided
- Monthly rent. Are there requirements as to how this is paid, for example by check, cash, money order?

  Some landlords require the rent to be paid through a debit card. If you do not have a debit card, there may be an additional fee added to your rent.

- Amount of the deposit to be held by the land-lord for any damages that occur
- If a lease is required and for how long?
- Any other special features about the location
- Phone numbers where you can reach the land-lord or property manager

Some ads include the address of the property or its general location and some do not. To find out where the property is located, it may be necessary to contact the owner or property manager at the phone number listed in the ad.

There are other questions listed below that you will want to ask of the person who is renting the property.

1. Is a deposit required to rent the property? If yes, how much is it and what needs to happen to be able to receive the deposit back once you terminate your lease on the property?

2. Who is responsible for the utilities?

(CAUTION)   If you as the tenant are responsible for paying utilities, you will need to pay a deposit to
the electric company, water department, and gas
company to have the monthly bills placed in your
name.

(Stop)   Remember to add these expenses to your
monthly budget.

3.   What is the average cost of utilities each month?

4.   Who is responsible for repairs at the residence?

5.   Who is responsible for mowing and trimming the
     yard?

6.   What furniture and appliances are provided by the
     owner, if any?

7.   Is there any additional storage space available with
     the property?

8.   Does the residence have central heat and air, or
     does it have window units and space heaters?

(CAUTION)   Window units tend to be much more expensive to operate.

9.   Is the yard fenced?

10. Is there a garage, covered parking, or a place to
     park your vehicle off of the road?

11. Do they allow pets, and is there a separate deposit for pets?

12. Will existing locks be replaced before you move in?

13. What can you tell me about the neighbors and the neighborhood?

14. Do you require rental insurance?

    Rental insurance is generally reasonable. If you have a computer and other valuables, you might want to consider obtaining this. Insurance companies that handle homeowners insurance generally provide rental insurance. Be sure to compare rates from several insurance companies.

15. Are there any rules that the landlord expects of the tenants?

16. How much notice is required of you when your lease is over and you are going to move?

17. Must notice of moving be in writing?

    If you would like to check further about the location of the property you are considering, you might contact the police department for crime statistics for the area in which you hope to rent. You might also check the website www.familywatch-dog.us. This site lists convicted sexual offenders who are living in the neighborhood where you are considering living.

Be sure to write down all of the information you obtain, including the address and the contact's phone number. Keep all of this information in a file folder so that you can easily refer to it.

If you are satisfied with the answers you receive, ask about meeting the owner to view the property. Some managers will want to meet you at the property or their office; others may leave the door to the rental unit open so that prospective tenants may look at the property and call back if they are interested in renting.

It is never safe to go into an unlocked property by yourself. Bring at least one friend with you.

As you view the property, observe the neighborhood, paying attention to how well other residents maintain their properties, and whether there is plenty of lighting on the street and around the house. What is the noise level like in the neighborhood? Make sure doors and windows lock, and that there is not any major damage to the property (holes in walls and floors, broken windows, or plumbing that needs repair).

Take a picture with your phone or camera showing any existing damage to the property so that you will not be held responsible for those repairs when you leave the property.

You may need to inspect many properties before you find the one that best suits you. Once you do, you are ready to notify the manager, agree to a move-in date, complete an application and sign any additional documents the landlord may require.

Applications

Many property owners and managers will require you to fill out an application so that they can obtain necessary information and check references before renting the property to you. You will probably be asked to fill out the application as soon as you view the property and decide you would like to rent it. The application will likely ask for the following information:

- Full name
- Current address
- Length of time you have resided at your current address
- Name of current or previous landlord or property manager
- Contact information for landlord or property manager
- Driver's license information (they may wish to make a copy of your license)
- Your contact information (cell phone)
- Name of employer
- Address of employer
- Phone number of employer
- Monthly income

 Some landlords require that your monthly income is two or three times the amount of the monthly rent of the property.

- Name of the bank where you do business
- Name of closest relative
- Contact information of relative
- Personal references with contact numbers
- Name of person who will be responsible for rent if you fail to pay (if you are under twenty-one)

Rental Agreements/Leases

The documents each manager requires tenants to complete vary a great deal. Usually you will need to sign a lease, deposit agreement, and pet deposit form (if applicable). The deposit for a rental is often the equivalent of one month's rent.

Be sure to read all documents thoroughly and ask questions if you do not understand something before signing these forms.

Some managers will ask you to inspect the property for damages and to complete a form noting the damages you observed.

Closely inspect the property for major things like damaged flooring, broken windows, and torn or stained carpet, but also note more minor things like holes in the walls where pictures hung.

Check to make sure any appliances that are provided by the owner are clean and in working order.

You will need to sign and date the inspection form. Ask for copies of *all* the forms you have completed.

If you notice damages, it's a good idea to take photographs with dates printed on them. These will be useful if you need to show the property manager that these damages occurred before you assumed responsibility for the property.

When you terminate your lease, the manager will inspect the property for any damages that have occurred during the time you leased the property.

The manager will take the money from your deposit to repair those damages or to have the apartment cleaned if you leave it dirty, and will then reimburse you whatever amount of money is left, if any.

When you decide to move from this property, the manager may also require *written* notice, usually thirty days in advance of your departure. Read your lease carefully to find out what you must do to have your deposit refunded.

CAUTION

You are also responsible for any damage caused by any of your visitors.

Once you have signed your lease, you will receive a set of keys to the property.

CAUTION

Immediately have two or three duplicate sets of keys made and keep them in a safe place apart from the residence. That way, if you ever leave your keys locked in your residence, you will have a way to get in. (Some rental managers charge as much as $50 to replace lost keys.)

Utilities

Now that you have a signed lease, you are ready to contact the utility companies to make deposits for whatever utilities you will be paying.

By calling or checking online you can determine exactly what information you will need to provide in order to place your deposit with the utility companies and have your utilities connected in your name. The information will generally include driver's license number and perhaps your Social Security number. If you are planning to move into your residence immediately and the utility company is unable to connect your services right away, be prepared to go without water, gas, or electricity for several days. In some cases, it may be a week or more before they can schedule a time to connect your utilities.

You will need to decide if it is necessary for you to have a traditional phone line and internet service. Some internet providers require that a home phone be installed before connecting service.

Now that you have completed the rental process, you are responsible for the care of the property and are ready to move in. You are ready to live on your own!

Resources

https://www.zillow.com
www.tulia.com
https://www.craigslist.org
www.familywatchdog.us.

6

Setting Up Your Own Place

> *One only needs two tools in life: WD-40*
> *to make things go and duct tape to make them stop.*
> — S. M. Weilacker

Furnishings/Appliances

Now that you have your own place, there are a number of items that you will need to make it comfortable. If you rented a furnished residence, many of these items may be provided.

If the appliances are included with your rental, the property manager is responsible for keeping them in good operating condition, and you should not have to pay for any repairs unless you caused the damage.

If you are providing the appliances, you will be responsible for keeping them operating. You will also have to move them out whenever you change locations.

Below is a list of some common items you may wish to have in your residence.

Kitchen:
- Stove/hot plate/griddle/microwave
- Pots and pans
- Refrigerator
- Glasses
- Plates
- Silverware
- Table and chairs
- Mixer
- Cooking utensils

Living room:
- Couch and chairs
- Window coverings
- Lamps
- Tables

Bedroom:

- Bed
- Plastic mattress cover
- Linens—sheets, pillows, pillowcases, and mattress pad
- Comforter or bed spread
- Lamps
- Bookcase
- Night stand

Bathroom:

- Shower curtain
- Towels
- Soap
- Toilet tissue
- Personal hygiene items
- Plunger

Miscellaneous

- Cleaning supplies
- Mop, broom
- Laundry detergent
- Clock
- Smoke alarm
- Carbon monoxide detector

It is imperative that you have enough smoke detectors to warn you if there is a fire. They can be purchased for a minimal price at most stores.

Batteries in smoke detectors should be changed twice a year. It is easy to remember to do this if you replace them whenever the time changes from standard time to daylight savings time and back again.

The expenses involved in purchasing all of these items may seem overwhelming at first. However, there are many places where you can purchase them cheaply.

Listed below are places you might shop to reduce the cost of setting up your place.

- Dollar Stores
- Garage sales
- Thrift shops
- Goodwill
- Salvation Army
- Relatives

You might also consider making some of the items. For example, you can create your own bookshelves by placing boards on top of concrete blocks. Cover the boards with fabric or paint to dress them up.

As you set up your residence you will find it very helpful to have a few tools handy. You will probably want a hammer, nails, screwdriver and screws, and picture hooks.

You may have to fix any holes you make!

Rental Insurance

Assuming that you are renting or leasing, the land-lord should carry insurance that covers the structure you are in should there be a fire or weather damage. However, that insurance will not cover your personal belongings.

Now that you are accumulating some belongings, you will want to consider rental insurance. This is particularly important if you own a computer, television, or other expensive electronics. Record and file in a safe place the serial numbers for electronic items, televisions, dvd players and other valuables.

Now is a great time to video tape all of your possessions and be sure that you put your name on your valuables. Use permanent marker or emboss your name so that no one can remove your identifying information.

Rental insurance is not mandatory, but ask yourself if you will be able to manage without your personal items, or if you can afford to replace them should they be stolen or suffer fire or weather damage.

If you decide that insurance is necessary, ask friends and relatives to recommend an insurance agent. Contact several different agents to obtain quotes on the various policies they offer.

Before speaking with any of the potential insurance agents, make a list of the valuables, including serial numbers, for items you want to insure and the approximate worth of those items. The agent will be better able to recommend the best coverage for your items if you have identified which ones you would like to insure.

Roommate Issues

Many people decide to share their residence with someone else, as this greatly reduces the expense of rent and utilities. However, you should only consider rooming with someone you feel you can trust, as living together can also lead to conflicts.

I strongly recommend that you discuss with your roommate how you will handle certain things. For instance:

1. Will the rent be split equally?

2. Who will be responsible for mailing or taking the rent to the landlord?

3. Will one person pay the rent with one check, then get the roommate's part of the rent from the roommate, or will each person pay the landlord separately?

4. The same question applies for utility payments.

5. Will you turn off utilities when no one is home in order to reduce expenses?

6. Who is responsible for cleaning? Will you set a day for cleaning and agree that each party will be there to complete the job?

7. Who will do the dishes?

    If you have only one plate and one glass each, the dishes will not stack up in the sink!

8. How will you deal with friends visiting?

9. Will you set a time after which all visitors should leave?

10. What if one roommate wants quiet time and the other wants to play music or watch television at a high volume?

11. Is trading or borrowing clothing acceptable?

12. Are pets allowed? (This may have already been decided by your landlord.)

Discussing potential issues *prior* to moving in with a roommate will greatly reduce the likelihood of problems developing. The time you spend discussing issues ahead may actually prevent the destruction of the friendship in the future.

Prior to moving in together, discuss how you

will handle unexpected issues. Will you agree to check with each other weekly to see if you need to discuss anything? Will you have a certain phrase you will use, such as "I am concerned," when you have something you would like to discuss with your roommate?

Now is a great time to put all of the decisions you have reached in the discussion with your roommate(s) into a written agreement. You may be great friends right now and think that this is a silly idea, but many friendships have ended over misunderstandings.

Terminating Your Lease

There are a number of reasons that you might decide to terminate your lease. It is best, if possible, that you do so at or after the completion of the lease agreement that you signed with your landlord.

Refer to the lease agreement you signed to see if you have stayed in this residence for the duration of the time to which you agreed. Also read carefully for any stipulations included in the agreement about how to terminate the lease.

Some leases require that you give thirty day's notice, and some landlords require you do this in writing.

If you do not follow all of the requirements in your lease you may lose all of your deposit even if your residence is immaculate when you leave.

The time frame allowed for the landlord to refund your deposit varies from state to state, but in some cases, the landlord has up to thirty days.

CAUTION

Be sure to leave the landlord a forwarding address so you can receive your deposit refund.

7

Handling Personal Responsibilities

There is an expiration date on blaming your parents for steering you in the wrong direction: the moment you are old enough to take the wheel, responsibility lies with you.

—J. K. Rowling

Now that you are on your own, there are many responsibilities you must assume. By being conscientious about meeting these responsibilities, you will have a much smoother trip on life's journey. Taking responsibility is another area where *you* are in charge of how well your trip goes. Until now, someone else has taken responsibility for providing your housing, food, and clothing, managing doctor's appointments, and other tasks necessary to keep you on the right road.

Driver's License

The steps for preparing, applying, and taking the test for a driver's license vary by state. You can obtain this information through the local office of your state department of motor vehicles. The information may also be available online. In Texas the website is txdmv.gov.

You are responsible for keeping your driver's license current. Typically, licenses are valid for either two or four years, depending on where you live. When your license expires you will be required to renew it. Generally, you can renew your license by filling out the necessary forms and paying the fee. Many states will mail the form to you before your license expires so that you can complete the form and pay the fee by mail by the designated date. In some states you are allowed to renew your driver's license online.

If you receive your first license at sixteen the renewal date may be as early as six months after receiving the license.

It is imperative that the vehicle you drive be licensed and insured. Be sure you have included this expense in your budget (see Chapter 1, Managing Finances).

In most states, a driver under the age of twenty-five can expect to pay much higher premiums for automobile insurance than those over twenty-five.

When you receive your driver's license you have tremendous responsibilities for your own safety and the safety of your passengers, as well as other drivers. You must take this responsibility very seriously.

There are many types of distracted driving that can increase the likelihood of accidents and fatalities. Some distractions that can occur while driving include eating, radios, drowsiness, texting, thinking about your next text and using a Global Positioning System (GPS). Having friends in the car can also increase distractions. It is critical that you devote your complete attention to your driving in order to be as safe a driver as possible.

Most states have laws that forbid people from texting while driving. Sending or receiving a text is not as important as your life or someone else's life. Be sure to pull over and stop at a safe location if you feel you must send or receive a text.

Bill Paying

Up until now, someone else has paid the bills. This is now your responsibility. Your bills *must* be paid on time to maintain a good credit rating. Many people pay bills on a specific date each month. If you are paid on the first of the month, that is a great day to pay bills.

If you are paid two times a month, you will need to determine which bills need to be paid with the first paycheck of the month and which bills can be paid with the second. The same is true if you are paid weekly.

Make a spreadsheet or chart of all bills that you have each month. The first column can show the person or business billing you. The next column can show the due date of the payment, and a third column can show the amount of the payment. Use this information to determine which bill is to be paid within which pay period.

You might also include a column showing the balance of that account so that you can watch your progress as you pay off your debt.

If you have a bill that must be paid once a year, it is a good idea to divide the amount due by twelve and put that amount into a savings account each month (or in an envelope if you are using the envelope system — see Chapter 1, Managing Finances). When that annual bill comes due you will already have the money set aside to pay for it.

Income Taxes

Now that you are employed, you will need to file income tax returns once a year. The due date each year is April 15. The forms you file will reflect the wages you earned and the deductions you paid during the previous calendar year. For example, forms filed on or before April 15, 2019, are for wages earned and deductions accrued from January 1, 2018, through December 31, 2018.

If you need help completing these forms contact a certified public accountant, the Internal Revenue Service, https://www.irs.gov or a private business like H & R Block, www.hrblock.com for assistance.

Registering for the Draft

If you are a male you are required to register for the draft through the Selective Service System, https://www.sss.gov when you reach the age of eighteen. You can do this by completing these forms online or obtaining the appropriate forms from your local post office or library. You must provide a valid driver's license or birth certificate.

You must provide address changes to the Selective Service System.

Registering to Vote

If you are eighteen, you are eligible to vote. You must register to vote in the county in which you live. You will need to fill out an application, which you can obtain through your county's election office. You may also register to vote at the time you apply for a new driver's license. Voting is a huge responsibility and it should not be taken lightly. Read about the candidates and watch televised debates to determine which candidate represents the values most similar to your own.

Self-Care

Taking care of yourself physically and emotionally is

an important component of being independent. It is important to have an annual health exam to prevent potential medical problems from arising or becoming worse.

Dental examinations are important for prevention as well. Dental professionals recommend that people have their teeth cleaned twice a year to prevent decay and other problems.

Some people may experience mental health issues. Should you feel depressed or are having difficulty handling daily tasks, the healthy thing to do is to visit a mental health professional—a licensed counselor, social worker, or psychologist.

There are several ways to locate qualified licensed professionals. Each state has licensing boards. They list professionals who have licenses in their states. Many communities have medical or dental organizations that can tell you who in your area is a member of their organization and is licensed.

Access to this information should be readily available online through your state Department of Health. It may tell you things like who maintains a current license and who has had complaints filed against them.

Another way of locating a qualified professional is by talking to friends and coworkers about who they would recommend. If you are a patient of a medical professional already, he or she may be willing to give you names of individuals who specialize in other areas.

Most cities have a referral service that can give you names of professionals and agencies located in your area. Many cities use the number 211 to connect people with needed services.

Community Service

Whether you realize it or not, from the time you were born people have been helping you out. They are at least partially responsible for who you have become and your success thus far.

When you were born, your mom and dad or primary caregivers were there to see that your needs were met. They started you on your journey to independence. As you continued your journey through life, there were probably other relatives, school teachers, music or dance teachers, coaches, Scout leaders, religious leaders, mentors, and friends who in some way gave of their time to influence who you are.

As you take charge of yourself and continue your journey to independence, one of your responsibilities is to decide how you might be willing to pay back some of the time and efforts that others gave to you.

You might be thinking, "There is nothing I can do for others," or "I don't have any particular skills," but often times, giving to others involves giving of your time and does not require a particular skill.

The first thing to think about in deciding how to give back is what population you might be interested in helping. Some of these might include young children, the elderly, those who are homeless, people who are ill, or those who are homebound.

Once you determine the population you would like to serve, you will find many agencies that will gladly receive your help. Most agencies have a wide variety of volunteer positions. The 211 phone number mentioned above might also be able to suggest organizations that are looking for volunteers.

If you think you might be interested in working with the elderly, you might visit a nursing facility for an hour a week and talk with the residents, read to them, or write letters for them.

If you are interested in working with children, you might contact the Boy Scout, Girl Scout, or Campfire offices in your community or any group residential facilities for youth that are located near you. You might be able to work with a small group of children or youth or do volunteer work in the agency's main office. Boys' clubs and girls' clubs often want volunteers to help with sports activities.

Some organizations and agencies in your community that might appreciate help are:

- Habitat for Humanity
- Boy Scouts of America
- Girls Scouts of the USA
- Goodwill
- Salvation Army
- Churches
- Food banks
- Homeless shelters
- Abuse shelters
- Schools
- Nursing homes
- Hospitals
- Mental health centers
- Child care centers
- Agencies that support people with specific diseases or disabilities; for instance, heart disease, cancer, muscular dystrophy, Down Syndrome, autism, etc. might also appreciate volunteers.

Community service can fuel your heart just as gasoline fuels your car. Helping someone else gives you satisfaction that can't be obtained in any other way. You are likely to meet some interesting people, and perhaps some will help you someday on your journey through life.

Volunteer work is a great item to include on your resume!

Resources

https://txdmv.gov.
https://www.irs.gov
https://www.hrblock.com
https://www.sss.gov
Call 211

8

Managing Your Time

The bad news is time flies.
The good news is you're the pilot.

—Michael Altshuler

Confusion and disorganization can represent very large potholes on your road to self-sufficiency. There are several simple tools that you can use to help keep yourself organized.

Calendars

Perhaps one of the **most** important tools you can use is a calendar. Some people will use calendars on their phones and/or computers and others will use calendars from office supply stores, department stores, or dollar stores. It does not matter what style of calendar you use, how large or small it is, or what color it is. The important thing is that you are comfortable with the type of calendar that you select. A calendar will help you keep your obligations organized.

It is a good idea to start by entering every activity that occurs on a regular basis—for instance, when your classes meet if you are a student, dates payments are due and birthdays. By doing this you will quickly discover what times are available to schedule other activities and appointments.

It is also good to schedule free time or time with friends on your calendar. That will help you in managing stress. (See Chapter 9, Managing Stress, for other stress management tips.)

Whether you are using a calendar on your computer, phone, or a paper calendar, try using colors to code your activities. For instance, you could put everything related to school in green, everything related to work in red, and fun activities in yellow.

If you are a student, include test dates and dates on which particular assignments are due. Some people find it helpful to also schedule times to prepare for tests or work projects. For instance, you could set aside prep time on June 3 for a presentation that is to be completed on June 10. This ensures that you will not be pulling an all-nighter the night before your project is due.

Other items to put on your calendar include reminders about friends' and family members' birth dates and anniversaries. You can note reminders for the specific event at the top of the date for that event and highlight that information so you will easily notice it.

Some people also include notes on their calendars about dates prescriptions need to be refilled, or dates when heater and air conditioner filters need to be replaced.

If you are using a calendar on your phone it will be easy to incorporate reminders by setting notifications of dates bills are due, birthdays and when assignments are due. I suggest that you google "apps for personal calendars". You will find lists of various apps and calendars for every purpose. The site www.capterra.com is a good site to review calendar software showing you the various features that are offered for different apps.

If you would like to include a birthday app as an organizational tool to remind you of friends' and family member's upcoming birthdays, you might try Birthday Calendar from the Apple App Store.

 There are many, many apps and websites available. It will be worth your time to research these and select the ones you feel will best suit your needs.

You may find it helpful to set some of the notifications several days in advance of dates bills are due, birthdays, etc. This allows you a little extra time to plan and you may find you are taking care of responsibilities ahead of time!

If you have a paper calendar, use a pencil to enter all of your activities. That way if a scheduled activity is cancelled or postponed, you can simply erase it instead of having to cross it out.

The only way a calendar will help you is if you use it. You must get in the habit of checking it daily. It may take a month or so to become accustomed to using a calendar on a regular basis, but if you practice using it, a calendar may soon become your best friend.

If you are using a calendar on your phone or computer, it is always a good idea to save your information frequently and to back it up in another location or make a printed copy of due dates, birthdays, and/or addresses in case your computer crashes.

Address Books

Although people do not use handwritten address books much anymore, I have found if my phone or computer crashes and I lose my information, I am very happy that I also saved this information in a handwritten address book.

As you journey through life, address books will become more and more important to you. They are an easy way to contact extended family members, old friends, business contacts, etc. You never know when you may need those addresses—for instance, for invitations to graduations, parties, weddings, or showers.

Your email program probably contains an address book. You can find printed versions of address books in some of the locations mentioned above that sell calendars.

As with your calendar, you will want to have a copy of addresses stored somewhere besides your phone or computer in case it crashes.

Setting Appointments

Now that you are managing your personal appointments on your own, there there will be many times when you need to set appointments. Some of these appointments might be to see a teacher, visit a doctor or dentist, meet with a potential employer, or talk to a landlord about renting an apartment. Whatever the appointment is, you want to remember it and be on time.

If you are late for a job interview, the employer will wonder how you will be able to make it on time to work. Being late could cost you a job! Do not over schedule yourself.

Allow travel time to get to appointments.

Most appointments are scheduled by telephone, text, or email. Always begin your contact with a friendly greeting. For example, "Hello, this is _____. May I please speak with _____? I would like to ask about setting an appointment [explain the reason for your call]." If you are speaking with a reception-ist or secretary and you are unable to speak directly with the person you wish to reach, ask the receptionist or secretary to take a message for you or connect you with the person's voicemail.

In your message, clearly state your name, the reason you are calling, and a number where the person may contact you. It is also helpful for you to tell this person when you will be available to receive a call. Thank the person you are speaking to for taking your message. It is much more likely that the person you are trying to reach will get your message if you are polite and friendly. If you are rude your message may end up in the trash.

Always speak clearly and slowly enough that the person is able to understand the information you would like to communicate.

Always say "Please" and "Thank you." This will

leave a much better impression with the person on the other end. Your manner of speaking is the only impression they will have of you.

Most people keep very busy schedules. Be sure that your phone is accepting messages in case they are unable to speak with you when they return your call. It is very frustrating to be unable to leave a message if the person does not answer their phone.

If you reach an incorrect phone number, always say something like, "I am sorry, I have the wrong number," or "I am sorry I interrupted you." It is very rude to just hang up without saying anything.

Arrange appointments so you can arrive five to ten minutes early. That way you will not appear rushed and frazzled.

Canceling Appointments

The courteous thing to do is to keep appointments you have scheduled. However, there are times when appointments must be cancelled. Should you need to cancel an appointment, do this as far in advance as possible so that someone else can use your appointment time.

Apply the same courtesies you did when you made the appointment, clearly stating your name and saying "Please" and "Thank you." Explain the reason for your cancellation and ask if there is a time available for you to reschedule.

Have your calendar available so that you can remove the original appointment time and enter the new time.

If you fail to cancel an appointment people will be hesitant to reschedule you as you have already cost them one time slot that someone else might have used. In some cases they will charge a fee to reschedule an appointment.

Making Lists

One of the most helpful methods of keeping yourself organized is making lists of the things you need to do. It is helpful to prioritize your list so that if you are unable to complete all of the tasks, you have at least taken care of the most important ones. You can then put the uncompleted items on the next day's list.

If you group items on your list by location, it saves you time and gas, and you may actually finish more of the to-do items.

Some people put their lists by their beds when they go to sleep. If they wake up during the night remembering something they need to do, they simply write it down and go back to sleep.

Structuring Your Environment

Now that you are on your own you will need to learn to manage all of the day-to-day things for which you are responsible. If you were getting ready to go on a trip, you would not drive your car in circles to get to your destination. You would map out the most efficient, direct route. This is what you also do to manage your time.

Some people can multitask (do several things at the same time), for instance wash clothes, cook dinner, and clean the house. Others are more efficient when they focus on one thing at a time. You will quickly figure out which way works best for you.

Whether or not you are someone who can multitask, you may find that you need help. Sometimes this help comes from others, and sometimes it comes from good organization and planning.

Ask friends and family members for any suggestions they may have regarding how they organize their days.

Below is a list of suggestions for managing your time.

1. Make a list of items you need from the grocery store so that you do not have to make frequent trips. Https://food52.com suggests you make a full list of items that you usually buy and then you can make multiple copies of this list. When you are

ready to shop you can refer to your list and check the items that you need. You can find a sample of their list on their website.

Some people find it helpful to arrange their grocery list in the order the items are located in their favorite grocery store.

2. When cooking meals, double the recipe and freeze half of it for another day.

3. If you are waiting for an appointment or waiting to pick someone else up, bring something to work on. For instance, study a textbook, revise your to-do list, or write a thank you note.

4. While you are doing laundry you might mend clothes, cook, or read.

5. Lay out your clothes the night before that you want to wear the next day so you are not running around the next morning looking for things or doing last-minute pressing. Some people lay out their clothes (including accessories) for the entire week.

6. If you just don't have time to wash dishes use paper plates.

7. Cut down on time spent on your computer or phone.

8. Watch less TV.

9. Learn to say no to things you do not want to do.

10. Get up thirty minutes earlier than you ususally do.

11. Go through all your mail at once, putting important items where they belong and discarding junk mail.

12. If it is difficult for you to get places on time, set your clocks and watches five minutes ahead.

13. Designate a place for everything and always return an item to its "home".

14. Group and contain similar items. Containing several small items that are used for the same purpose can be placed together. Examples might be things you need to sew or mend clothes or school supplies.

15. If you are a student or an employee who works from home, designate a space that is where you study or work. It needs to be a quiet space away from the activities that go on in your home. Any paper work, books, etc. associated with school or work can be organized in this space so that items do not get misplaced.

Resources

www.capterra.com
https://food52.com

9

Managing Stress

> *If you ask what is the single most important key to longevity, I would have to say it is avoiding worry, stress, and tension. And if you didn't ask me, I'd still have to say it.*
>
> —George Burns

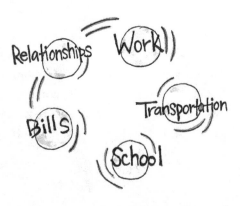

As you know, it is important to watch for any signs that indicate that your vehicle is having problems. Perhaps the warning lights on your dashboard come on, you smell something heating up, or hear an unusual noise. These signs would tell you that something is not working correctly and that your vehicle needs attention. Failure to give attention to these warning signs can result in much more serious damage to your vehicle, and might even result in your being unable to get where you are going.

This same concept applies to your body and your mind as you continue on your journey to independence. Everyone suffers from stress at various times. Sometimes the stress is greater than usual. As with your vehicle, there are early warning signs to indicate that you might be affected by stress. It is very important to learn to recognize the signs your body gives to you, and to take action to manage your stress so that you do not become incapable of managing your personal relationships or your job.

Causes

Stress is generally an adaptation to change. It can be caused by any number of things. What stresses one person may not stress another. You may experience extreme stress in response to a situation that makes your friend only mildly concerned. Stress can be positive or negative. Positive stress will actually cause some people to function better, while negative stress may cause people to become frustrated or shut down and be unable to handle their daily activities.

Frustration may arise when you feel inadequate or unable to cope. It may result from an obstacle in the way of a goal, lack of control over work, or a delay in receiving a reward.

Almost anything can be a stressor, depending on how you perceive it. Perhaps you have been given a promotion at work for which you worked very hard. Even though this is a positive situation, it might still result in a great deal of pressure and stress. Perhaps you are concerned about whether or not you can handle the new position, or whether your coworkers will be jealous of you.

Other changes might be going back to school, moving away from a familiar location, changing jobs, breakup of a relationship, or health issues. These are all situations that can cause stress, but again, no two people are stressed by the same situations in the same way.

As you deal with change there might be mental, physical, or emotional signs of stress.

Signs

The signs of stress differ greatly from one person to another. It is important to become aware of *your* early signs so that you can manage the stress in your life and avoid some of the consequences of unmanaged stress that are discussed below.

Signs of stress can be physical, emotional, and behavioral. Some of the signs that people have identified are:

1. Physical
    *   Headaches
    *   Stomachaches

- Intestinal problems
- Heart racing or pounding
- High blood pressure
- Migraine headaches
- Pain in neck and back
- Grinding of teeth
- Trembling
- Fatigue
- Dryness of throat
- Insomnia

2. Emotional
   - Irritability
   - Unexplained anxiety
   - Restlessness
   - Depression
   - Emotional instability
   - Feelings of hopelessness
   - Feelings of helplessness

3. Behavioral
   - Impulsivity
   - Inability to concentrate
   - Loss of appetite
   - Excessive appetite
   - Alcohol or drug use
   - Accident proneness
   - Physical or verbal attacks
   - Causing harm to oneself or others

You may find that you experience only a few of these signs, or perhaps many. In either case, the earlier you recognize them and begin to manage your stress, the better your health will be.

Consequences

Stress that goes unmanaged will continue to do damage to your body just as problems with your car that are not repaired will do greater damage to your vehicle. Untreated stress can lead to many of the following disorders and diseases:

- High blood pressure
- Heart disease
- Stroke
- Diabetes
- Asthma
- Hives
- Tension headaches
- Migraine headaches
- Cancer

Everyone deals with stress in their lives. The earlier you recognize the signs of stress and manage the stress, the fewer long-term effects you are likely to experience.

Techniques to Manage Stress

There are a number of techniques you can use to manage stress. You may need to try several of these before you decide which ones are the most effective for you.

- Breathe deeply. Take in a deep breath and hold it to the count of ten, then slowly release it.

  This can be helpful if you are about to speak in front of a group of people or interview for a job. (No one can even tell when you are doing this.)

- Smile inwardly. Think of something that is pleasant to you but keep it to yourself.

- Use imagery. Visualize something pleasurable, perhaps a place you have been or the face of a friend.

- Practice progressive muscle relaxation. Start at the top of your head. Relax your facial muscles for several minutes, then relax your neck muscles, and continue working down your body.

- Pretend there are holes in the bottom of your feet. (I know this sounds crazy.) Take a deep breath and bundle all your worries into this breath. Slowly release your breath and pretend your worries are escaping through the holes in your feet.

- Eat sitting down instead of standing.

- Practice self-talk. Instead of mentally saying, "I will never pass this test," or "I will never do this job well," say, "I am just as good as anyone else," or "I am going to do my very best." *You* are in charge of your own thoughts.

- Exercise, exercise, exercise. Walking or running not only does wonders for your physical health, but also clears out the cobwebs in your brain.

Walking or running a mile is equivalent to 5 mg of Valium.

- Adjust your diet. Avoid sugar and caffeine. Try some of the foods listed below.
  - Bran
  - Brown rice
  - Peanut butter
  - Tuna
  - Spinach
  - Milk
  - Chicken
  - Green peas
- Eat four to five small meals a day.
- Increase your calcium intake (it acts as a tranquilizer).
- Set aside fifteen to thirty minutes of quiet time a day.
- Enjoy the sunset.
- Do something for yourself each day, even if it is only for five minutes.
- Get plenty of sleep.
- Talk out worries with a friend.
- Accept what can not be changed.
- Do something for others.
- Get a hobby
- Perform community service
- Take a vacation
- Delegate certain activities to a family member
- Listen to or play music
- Pray

Resources

https://www.skillsyouneed.com/ps/stress-tips.html

10

Ensuring Safety and Security

> *A prudent man foresees the difficulties ahead and prepares for them; the simpleton goes blindly on and suffers the consequences.*
>
> Proverbs 22:3

When taking a trip, you want your car to run well to avoid accidents and to complete your journey safely. You can do this by taking precautions to see that your car is full of gas and well tuned, the tires are properly inflated, and you have directions to your destination.

On your road to independence, it is also necessary to take various precautions so that your journey is a safe one.

Unfortunately, the world is not always a safe place to

be. Since you are in charge, it is up to you to be aware and cautious when you are at home or out in the community. Being alert to your environment and the people around you is one of the most important things you can do to keep you, your family, and your friends safe.

The precautions discussed below are not intended to scare you, but to keep you—not someone else—in charge or your environment and safety.

Precautions at Home

Now that you have your own residence, ask the landlord if the locks were changed after the last tenant lived in your residence.

If the landlord has not changed the locks, request that this be done as quickly as possible. It is very easy for previous tenants or their friends to make multiple keys, giving them easy access to where you now live.

Below are some suggestions that may keep you safe at home:

1. Check to see that all windows and doors have working locks, and always be sure you keep these locked, even when you are at home.

    This applies to anywhere you live, including a school dormitory. Break-ins occur daily all across the country. You do not want to be surprised to find someone entering your residence for the wrong reasons.

2. If you are leaving your home and expect to return after dark, leave a light or two on inside so it appears that someone is home.

    You might want to put timers on lamps in your residence. The timers can be programmed to turn off and on at set times, making it appear that someone is moving around inside.

3. Have security lights mounted around the residence. There are several types of security lights. Photocells come on when it gets dark and go off when it is light outside. These are very helpful if you often leave during the day and return after dark. Solar lights can be placed outside. They operate off of energy from the sun.

    If you have had several rainy days in a row, your outside solar lights may not provide any light as they are powered by sunlight.

4. Another type of security light is a motion detector. The light comes on whenever movement occurs within a certain distance of the detector.

5. Keep shrubs trimmed away from doors and windows so that it is difficult for anyone to hide around your residence.

6. Whenever you approach your door from the outside, have your key in your hand, ready to unlock the door.

Your key can also be used as a weapon, if necessary.

7. Always be aware of your surroundings. Look alert and look around. Do not distract yourself by talking on your cell phone or digging in a purse or bag. Act like you are in charge.

8. If you have a subscription to a newspaper and you are planning to be out of town, temporarily cancel that subscription so that you do not have papers gathering outside your house. This is like a flashing sign to prowlers saying no one is home.

9. The same is true for your mail. If your mail is delivered to a mailbox outside your home instead of a mail slot that allows the mail to go directly inside, you will want to stop the mail delivery while you are out of town. You can go to the post office or go online at www.usps.com to have your mail temporarily stopped. You will need to provide the exact dates that you want to stop mail delivery and resume it.

10. Install working smoke alarms in your residence. These can save your life should you ever have a fire. Smoke alarms are available for many different prices and can be found in discount stores and home improvement stores. Generally people install them in the cooking area and bedrooms. It is *critical* to have working alarms in your residence.

 Remember to change the batteries in smoke

alarms about every six months. A good way to re-member this is to change the batteries when the time changes from daylight savings time to stan-dard time and back to daylight savings time.

11. If you have gas in your residence or a working fire-place, also install a carbon monoxide detector.

12. Keep a working flashlight by your bed in case the electric power goes off in your residence.

Precautions Away from Home

Many people become preoccupied when they leave home. They may be thinking about meeting their friends, all of the things they have to accomplish that day, or someone or something that is important in their lives. Keep these tips in mind.

1. Be aware of your surroundings. Note anyone who looks suspicious.

    A person does not have to look grubby or shabby to be dangerous. Someone who is very clean and nicely dressed could also harm you.

2. If you are leaving the mall, school, or work at night, leave with someone else, if possible.

3. *Trust your gut!* If you get that funny feeling that something is not right, find a safe person or loca-tion immediately.

4. Keep your car keys in your hand.

5. Lock your car doors even when you are in your car.

6. Do not sit in your car at the mall or a public place and work on your checkbook or to-do lists; you may become unaware of what is going on around you.

7. *Never* get in a vehicle with a stranger.

8. Keep your purse or bag across your shoulder or close to your body so that it cannot be grabbed.

9. If it is necessary to use your cell phone, continue to look around you and be aware of others and what they are doing.

10. Have a plan for what you will do if someone approaches you or tries to grab you.

Karate studios and some police departments offer classes to help you prepare for the unexpected.

11. If you like to exercise out-of-doors, have someone go with you. Be aware of your surroundings, and select open, well-lit areas. . You may want to consider taking a container of spray mace with you. Mace is very inexpensive but might be very helpful. If you have mace, you can spray this in the face of someone who is trying to grab or hurt you. Mace will burn their face and especially someone's eye so that they will be temporarily incapacitated. This will allow you extra time to run to a safe place.

12. When you are socializing and have a drink, alco-

holic or not, keep your drink in your hand. If you have to set it down and leave to do something, do not drink any more of that drink. It is easy for someone to put something in your drink that makes you very sick or unable to control your actions.

There are various drugs that can be put into a drink unnoticed and undetected. They can cause memory loss and impair the ability to fight off an attacker.

There are several gadgets available that can detect some rape drugs. If you look online at the site https://efficientgov.com you will find information about cups, straws, nail polish, and coasters that are developed or being developed that may be able to detect some date rape drugs in a drink. These items may not detect all date rape drugs. Please research these gadgits online to learn the pros and cons of each item. Some of these gadgits are available at www.amazon.com.

Precautions While Traveling

A trip is generally most successful when you have made careful plans. Try following the precautions below to avoid having difficulties on the road. It will make your expedition much more enjoyable.

1. Before leaving on your trip, be sure that your vehicle is in good working condition. Have the oil and fluids checked, as well as the tires.

2. Learn how to change a flat tire. Have a cell phone with you to be able to call for help. Be sure it is fully charged. Make sure that the tire jack in your car is in good working condition and that your spare tire has plenty of air.

    Some states print an emergency number for the Department of Public Safety on your driver's license. Check to see if your license has an emergency call number on it. If so, you can call that number for help should you experience trouble on the highway. Some insurance companies and AAA offer roadside services for a fee.

    Pack your cell phone charger with you so you will always be able to use your phone when in range of a cell tower.

3. Keep a bag of tools with you, including a hammer, screw driver, pliers, expandable wrench, flares, flashlight, and wire.

    It is a good idea to also take an umbrella and rain tarp in case you have car trouble during bad weather.

    Having a blanket to kneel or lie on while working on your car can be very helpful.

4. Take a map of your route and decide ahead of time how you are going to get there. This will save time and gas and keep you from wandering into

unknown and perhaps unsafe locations. Google Maps, https://maps.google.com, and MapQuest, https:mapquest.com, are great tools for obtaining directions and maps to route you to your destination. There are also apps available for your phone. A popular app is Yelp, www.yelp.com. Not only does Yelp help with directions, it can help you locate restaurants, gas stations and places of interest.

Be sure that someone you trust has a copy of your travel information in case of an emergency. This information would include the directions you are traveling, where you are staying and your ultimate destination. Also, include when you plan to leave home and return. This may be very helpful if your car breaks down, you are stranded in an area that has no cell phone coverage or you run into other difficulties.

Occasionally these services may be wrong, so check their directions on another map to make sure they are accurate.

5. Be sure you have plenty of gas.

Always fill up before your gas gets below a quarter of a tank. That way you never need to walk to a gas station or to get help.

6. If you are staying in a hotel or motel, make your reservations ahead so you are assured of a room for the night.

7. Keep water, snacks, a blanket, and a first aid kit in your car. Even if you have planned carefully, unexpected events such as construction, weather problems, or an accident on the highway can significantly delay you.

General Precautions

It is wise to always keep emergency phone numbers easily accessible. If you have a cell phone, program "911" as well as emergency contact numbers into it. Some people store a phone number identified as "ICE" ("in case of an emergency") in their cell phone address books for others to be able to contact a family member if necessary. Others may enter "home" in the address book. These numbers can be helpful if you lose your phone. The person who locates it can find you through your phone's contact list.

It is also wise to include in your phone the number of an emergency room or pharmacy in the locations where you will be traveling.

Whether or not you have a cell phone, it is a good idea to keep a written copy of important numbers with you and at home. Some people use small address books and keep them in their purses or back packs or in a safe place at home. If the battery on your phone dies or your phone crashes you will have these important numbers in another location.

Whenever you enter your car, always check the back

seat to be sure that no one unexpected has climbed in your car. This could be animals, small children or strangers. This applies to brief stops as well, like when you get out to fill up your car with gas.

Resources

https://www.usps.com
https://efficientgov.com
www.amazon.com.
https://maps.google.com,
https://www.mapquest.com,
www.yelp.com

11

Succeeding in School

Self-esteem comes from achievements,
not from lax standards and false pride.

—Condolessa Rice

Gaining an education can be an important tool for you as you continue your journey toward independence. At times it may feel that pursuing an education is like traveling up a mountain. There may be curves, bumps, and obstacles in the road. You might look out over the edge of the mountain side and think you are never going to make it to the top of the mountain.

Fortunately, there are many keys to learning and studying that can make this journey much easier.

Attendance

Attending class is critical to being successful in school. Make school a priority. If you are not in class, you do not hear the material discussed, know when an assignment is due, or know when the next test will be given.

Some instructors will allow you a certain number of absences with no penalty. These absences are for you to use when needed. However, using absences early in the semester because you would like a day off or would like to sleep late is *not* a good idea. If several absences are taken at the beginning of the semester, it appears to the instructor that school is not a priority to you.

CAUTION

Some instructors take points off of your grade average at the end of the semester for each absence. Points being taken off can quickly cause a low "A" to become a "B".

Always contact your instructor if you are going to be late or miss a class session. Many instructors are much more lenient if they understand your situation. Communication with your instructors is critical for success.

You may become ill during the semester or have another emergency arise causing you to be absent from class. You want to save your absences for these situations.

STOP

Having broken up with your boyfriend or girlfriend is *not* a good reason to miss classes. If you take all of the allotted absences for these types of reasons, and then you become ill, the instructor may not have much sympathy for you. They may still deduct points for the absences you now take even though you might actually be ill because you already used up all of the absences that were given to you.

CAUTION
   If you are sleeping in class you may be counted absent or asked to leave the class.

After missing class, upon your return to class do not ask the instructor if there is "anything I missed". This sounds to the instructor as though you think nothing important occurs in his or her class.

CAUTION
   Be sure to get the notes you missed from other students. Teachers do not want to repeat lectures they have already given.

It will be helpful to get phone numbers of several students early in the semester so that you can contact them to make copies of notes and check on assignments that you may have missed when you were out of class.

Classroom Behavior

Your behavior in the classroom can greatly impact your relationship with your instructor. You want to leave the impression that you care about the class and want to perform well in order to earn a good grade.

Having a positive attitude about your classes is a major factor in being successful in school.

Below find a list of things you can do to keep organized and leave a favorable impression with your instructor. Some of these suggestions sound very basic, but are often overlooked.

- Arrive at class 5 minutes early.
- Sit at the front of the class.

CAUTION

If you arrive to class late or must leave early, take a seat at the back of the room so as not to disturb others. If you must leave early, inform your instructor before class begins. Do not interrupt class to tell your instructor you are leaving.

- Have pens and paper ready when the lecture begins.
- Always put your name and the name of the class on your papers.
- Work only on assignments for the class you are attending, not assignments for other classes.
- Use a different notebook for each class.
- Some people like to color code each of their classes (red is math, green is English, etc.). Use this color to cover your text book, for the notebook you use to record notes and anything else related to the class.
- If you take a laptop to class use it to take notes not to check email or surf the internet.

Date your class notes and number the pages to help you keep information organized.

Indicate in your notebook where the notes for one test end, and the new test material begins.

- Buy the required book for the class and READ it!
- If the instructor has provided a calendar or handouts regarding assignments for class, you should check these before arriving at class so that you are always prepared for class.
- Turn in assignments on time.

Many instructors take points off for late assignments regardless of the quality of the work.

- If there are several pages to one assignment, either paper clip or staple the papers together. Do not expect your instructor to keep up with loose pages.

Be sure your name is on every page just in case the pages get separated.

- When a test or assignment is returned, record the grade in the front of your notebook. That way you will always be able to calculate your grade average in that class.

- If you have a question, be sure to ask it. You are probably not the only student wondering the same thing.

Do *not* talk during class while the instructor or other students are talking.

Do *not* sleep in class.

Do *not* text on your cell phone or run out of the room to take a call while class is in session.

Do *not* put on make up or perform personal grooming tasks during class.

If you determine what is important to your instructor and what the instructor's pet peeves are, you are more likely to do well in class.

Study Habits

You can do many things outside of class to help you prepare for class time, assignments, and tests that will help you improve your grades. Some suggestions are listed below:

- Read your assignments ahead.

  Many students find it helpful to highlight or underline important material as they read.

- After you have left class, retype or rewrite your notes to help you become familiar with the information.
- Read through your notes each night to become more comfortable with the material.

If you read your notes between classes and there is something you don't understand, you will have an opportunity to ask the instructor questions about those notes before test day.

- Study as soon after class as possible.
- Study your most difficult course first while you are the freshest.
- Take 10 minute breaks every hour or so.
- Create a place to study that is your space. Always put your back pack, books, etc. in your study area so you don't have to search for them.
- Study at the same time each day.
- Study three hours after class for every one hour you spend in class
- Study in groups with other class members if you find group studying is beneficial for you.
- Reread all written assignments at least once or twice to catch any errors you might have made.
- Then read your paper out loud as this may help you find any other errors you may have missed while reading.

 Always keep extra printer paper and ink available so you will not need to make a late night run to the store.

- Some students learn well by transferring their class notes to index cards. You can write a question on the front of a card and the answer on the back to test yourself while studying for an exam.

Make holes in the corner of your note cards and place them on a ring. This way you can conveniently carry them with you.

Take your index cards or class notes with you to run errands or go to appointments. If you get stuck in traffic or have to wait anywhere you will be able to get in a little studying while waiting.

When you have completed your studying for the day, put your books and back pack in the car to save time in the morning.

Test Taking

Be prepared with pens and pencils when taking a test. Some instructors will require you to record your answers on a printed form. The answers must be recorded with a #2 pencil in order for the answers to be read by the machine that is grading the form.

Some students experience test anxiety or are unable to test well under standard classroom conditions. This information should be shared with your instructor. He or she will work with you to accommodate any special needs you may have.

CAUTION
When taking a test, if you do not know the answer, guess. You might earn several points for your answer even if you don't get full credit.

CAUTION
If you don't understand a question on your test be sure to ask the instructor for clarification.

Read all of the possible answers in multiple choice test questions before choosing your answer.

Always attempt bonus questions. Any extra points you earn may make a significant difference in your grade at the end of the semester.

Do not take your test late. Putting it off because you think you will do better if you have more time to study rarely works for students.

CAUTION
If you miss a test and try to take it later, you may find that is not allowed or that there will be points taken off of the test grade you actually earned.

By paying attention to the above suggestions you will find that furthering your education may not be as difficult as you may have imagined. Once people learn skills that make school easier they often find that they want to gain more education than they ever imagined they would. Learning can be fun and very beneficial. It can enhance your credentialing, job position, and your self-esteem. It feels very satisfying when you reach the top of the mountain!

Furthering Your Education

Now that you have successfully completed high school or received your General Education Diploma (GED) you may be considering furthering your education. There are several options available. Community colleges offer one year certificates (30 credit hours) and two year associate degrees (60 credit hours). In some majors you may be job-ready with a one year certificate.

Once someone has earned a certificate, they may decide to earn a two year associate degree. The 30 credit hours from the one year certificate will generally be credited toward a 60 credit hour associate degree, if the certificate is in the same field of study as the associate degree.

The next step on the educational ladder is a bachelor's degree, commonly called a four year degree. After earning that degree a student may choose to earn a master's degree and then a doctoral degree.

CAUTION   It is possible that someone is not really interested in a traditional college degree, but wants to attend a technical college where they become trained with particular job skills. The length of time for this educational step varies from one field of study to another.

Credit hours are the number of "college credit" hours you have earned. College level courses usually are 2, 3, or 4 credit hour courses. Each credit hour is equal to 16 clock hours.

This information can be very confusing and can differ from one educational institution to another. Therefore, it is very important that you speak with a representative from the school that you wish to attend. If you are uncertain where you would like to continue your education, it is very important that you visit various schools and talk with representatives of each school. This will often make your decision very clear.

From here the exact steps each school requires may be a little different from one another, however, some things are similar. First of all, gather general information from each school about the program(s) in which you are interested. This information may help you make a decision about where you want to attend if you are still confused.

Some people may still be confused about where they would like to receive their education. They may decide to apply to several schools.

You will be asked to submit an application, usually on-line, and request that an official transcript from your high school or a copy of your GED be sent to the school to which you would like to attend.

Be prepared for the school to request several more things. You may be asked to take a placement test in English, Writing and Math to determine if you need developmental course work in order to be successful in furthering your education. You may be asked to complete health forms and other documents that are specific to your school choice.

Another important decision will be how you intend to pay for your classes. This is sometimes scary to think about and for some people it seems impossible to answer. I encourage you to explore payment options with the Financial Aid Office at your school.

One of the first things the financial aid office will ask you to do is complete a form called FASFA. This stands for Free Application for Federal Student Aid. You will complete this form online at https://fafsa.gov. It will be necessary for you to complete this form to determine your eligibility for grants, loans and scholarships.

Ask if your school has someone who can be of assistance with these forms, if necessary. You will need a copy of your income tax return and your parents' tax return, as well as other financial information. It will be important to know someone to whom you can ask questions because you want to complete this form correctly. If there are errors in completing the form, there will be delays in approving you for financial aid. Some people are actually delayed starting school due to errors on this form.

Once your FASFA form and your school application are submitted you will anxiously wait to hear that you have been accepted.

Once you are accepted, you will be informed of the orientation and advising processes for your school. A part of these processes will include choosing your classes and actually registering for them. Your school will explain all of these steps to you.

Below are some tips to help you be successful at your chosen school.

1. Memorize your Student Identification Number (Student ID)

2. Once you are registered in classes be sure to keep a copy of your class schedule in your school notebook where you can easily find it.

3. Explore the school's website. Figure out how to access your class schedule and degree plan (showing all of the courses you need for your degree).

4. Before the first day of classes review your schedule carefully to know when and where your classes meet.

5. Before classes begin, make a trip to campus to locate the buildings and rooms in which your classes will be held so that you can arrive at classes on time.

6. If you have classes at multiple locations on campus actually walk or drive your class schedule so that you know how long it will take you to go from one class to another so that you will be at class on time.

7. Be sure you have your supplies and books together and decide how you are going to carry those around campus, i.e., backpack, tote bag, etc.

8. Supplies should include pens, pencils, highlighters, and separate notebooks or pocket folders for each class. You might also want subject dividers, a small stapler, and paper clips. Individual instructors may require additional materials.

9. Refresh yourself on the tips found earlier in this chapter about how to succeed in school.

10. Keep in mind that you have taken a big step by enrolling in higher education, but you are in charge! You have the tools to be successful!!!!

If you feel confused or need help, you will find that most schools have many, varied resources to help you succeed. All you need to do is ask someone for help. Ask your instructors, your student advisor, and/ or your classmates. Find a student who was in your school last year. Everyone was new at this process at one time and had many of the same questions you may have.

If these educational options do not appeal to you, perhaps you would like to pursue a military career. There are recruiting offices for all of the branches of service. Each branch will have its own recruiting office so you may want to google the Army, Navy, Marine Corps, and Coast Guard to learn about each of these branches of service. Online you can also find tips for visiting the recruiting offices at https//www.military.com/join-armed-forces/recruiting-10-tips.html

Resources

- https://fafsa.gov
- http://www.military.com/join-armed-forces/
- https://opportunity.org/learn/lists/10-habits-of-successful-students#.WyPGkWNOlpg

12

Handling Social Issues and Relationships

This is your life. You are responsible for it.
You will not live forever. Don't wait.
—Natalie Goldberg

As you travel the road to independence you may find that there will continue to be bumps and pot holes in the road. There will be various issues that you and/or your friends may need to face and solve. Please keep in mind that discussing these situations and issues is not intended to scare or worry you.

If you think about a situation before it happens and think about possible solutions, you will be more likely to handle it an effective way. Keep in mind that there is *always* a solution to problems. Some solutions are better that others, but there is always an answer.

You are in charge and can make changes happen. You have many decisions to make.

Friendships, Dating and Social Media

As you were growing up you may have had many friends. Probably you met these people through school, church, scouts, sports and other activities that perhaps you were exposed to by your parents.

Think back on how you met someone in sports. You both showed up, maybe one of you said "hello." You may have started talking about the sport you were joining, the coach, or practice. After repeated interactions with this person maybe you realized you had a great deal in common. Each time you met for practice or a game, you had more and more to talk about. Eventually you realized things about this person that you liked. Maybe they were outgoing, friendly, or reliable. You both mutually contributed to this friendship and it may have lasted for years.

Now that you are on your own, you may be in situations where you are meeting many new people and forming new friendships. Of course this doesn't mean you need to give up old friends, but you do need to think about the possibility of new friendships and how these are formed.

Some of the ways people meet others, make friends and form relationships today can be very different from how it was when you were a child. Now people are often introduced or find each other online. Sometimes this is through a mutual friend. Sometimes people are connected by online websites. In either case, it is important to develop relationships over time.

If you are introduced to someone through social media, you learn about them through electronic means. Some social media sites will vet their users to try to determine the accuracy of their personal information. This may help you gain information about the person you might want to meet face-to-face.

Keep in mind that just because information is on someone's online profile, it doesn't mean that it is accurate. Some people include information that they think others want to hear, but is not really true about them. Profiles can easily be made up. IF you decide you want to meet this person face-to-face, you don't want surprises about who they are.

Be sure to talk on the phone several times to begin to get to know each other.

Talking on the phone may help you get an idea of the true gender and age of this person and whether or not the online profile describing them is accurate. (Online a person can say anything. They might say they are female when actually they are male.)

Remember that when talking on the phone, you are not able to see any non-verbal messages the person may be giving. (Non-verbal messages include smiling, frowning, making gestures, shrugging shoulders or anything that does not include words.) Maybe they are grinning because they are making up information or they think that they are about to convince you of something untrue.

You can begin communicating with this person through disposable email addresses or disposable phones. This may sound silly, but if this person ends up being a stalker, it will be much easier to lose them if they know you only through a disposable means. This also can keep them from identifying your location if you do not want them to know where you are.

Before meeting this person, you want to learn as much about them as possible. Try to find out where they live, where they go to school or work and if you have any mutual friends.

You do want to be cautious about building friendships, however, as there are obviously some people who are not good choices to have as friends.

At no time in any relationship is sexting (texting inappropriate sexual messages or photos to someone) a good idea. It may seem ok at the moment, but remember, unintended people may see the photos or messages. If the recipient of the messages gets mad at you or ends your relationship, they may send the information to others whom you do not want to see this information.

 Once pictures are posted on social media or anywhere else online, it is almost impossible to remove that information. Those party pics may include people and activities that you do not want seen in the future.

Some people have had difficult times obtaining jobs because of inappropriate material that was posted online about them and later was seen on the internet by potential employers.

Many powerful people have lost jobs and lucrative careers because information they intended for one person only was unknowingly shared with others.

Once you feel comfortable setting up a meeting with someone you have met online, consider taking a friend with you to the meeting. If you choose not to do this, be sure to let your friends and/or family know where you will be meeting. You can share your location on your smartphone so that family or friends can track you, if necessary. An app named Moby, found online at https://itunes.apple.com.us/app/moby/id394144982?mt=8   is one of several apps that can be used so that others can know where you are at all times.

Any meeting you agree to should take place in a

restaurant, or a very public place where there are lots of other people around you. By doing this you should be able to call out for help if you feel uncomfortable with this person.

Take a picture of this person and also take a picture of their vehicle, (including the license plate, if possible). This applies if you are a male or female. Consider meeting in a busy, public place three or four times to learn more about this person before deciding to be alone with them.

If at any time you feel uncomfortable with this person or feel they are trying to control you or are not being respectful of you, TRUST YOUR GUT. That means if you get that creepy or uncomfortable feeling in your stomach, pay attention to that. It is probably a good idea to end that relationship right away.

Never share your email passwords with people you meet online (or with friends). Even though you may feel very close to someone, this is private information. If your relationship with this person ends, they would still have access to your financial information, credit and other personal identification.

EVERYONE deserves to be treated with respect. Your feelings and opinions matter. No one has the right to control you or have things only their way. Relationships should be equal.

Many people as young as 15-16 years of age have been in situations in which an ex-boyfriend or ex-girlfriend has stalked them after a breakup. Sometimes these relationships are very difficult to end. (See more below regarding domestic violence.)

I realize that you may feel that some of these suggestions are silly or way too much to worry about. As a mental health professional, a parent, and a grandparent, I am aware of many situations in which people wish they had followed this advice.

There are abductions and murders that occur daily. In some instances, this happened because relationships were formed without knowing much about the other person. This person turned out to be very dangerous.

There are situations where people have met online and formed healthy, long lasting relationships. Those situations seem to occur more frequently when the people involved are very mature and have had experience in dating and developing interpersonal relationships.

When you develop a relationship with someone, either online or in person, you may eventually decide that this is not a relationship you want to continue.

Some reasons you might want to end a relationship include:

1. Your life revolves completely around the other person.

2. This person humiliates you or verbally insults you.

3. There is ever physical violence.

    Whenever there is physical violence, you can expect that it will happen again, be more severe and more frequent (even if the person who does the abusing says they will never do this again).

4. Your partner tries to control who you see, what you do, where you go and how you dress.

5. They are moody or have emotional outbursts (generally just at you).

6. They keep you away from your friends and family and want you to only spend time with them.

7. They are very jealous.

8. They ask you to change the way you dress or to wear less makeup when you are around others.

9. You or your friends or family members have concerns about your relationship.

These signs should raise red flags for you, indicating that this may not be a healthy relationship.

Once you decide a relationship is unhealthy, you need to decide once and for all that you are going to end the relationship and not go back. *It will not get better.*

Generally people do not change the ways they relate to others. So make a clean break.

It is time to create a safety plan. Who will you be with, where will you stay, do you need to let employers or teachers know of your situation?

Listed below under Domestic Violence are tips about the items to include in a grab bag, in case you need to leave in a hurry.

If you haven't already, it is now time to let family and friends know about your decision to leave this person. Let people you trust help you through the process of leaving.

During the time someone is ending a relationship is often when more severe abuse or even death may occur. You want others around you to keep you safe.

It rarely works to try to maintain a friendship with someone with whom you are no longer in an intimate relationship. It is best to completely separate from this person.

Resources

- https://itunes.apple.com.us/app/moby/ id3941449?mt=8 app to identify your location

- https://www.cbsnews.com/news/tips-for-vetting-your-online-dates/

- https://lifehacker.com/.../how-to-use-the-internet-to-investigate-your-next-date-co-wor...

Domestic Violence

NO ONE has the right to hurt you or anyone else, physically, emotionally, sexually or financially. If this behavior occurs with someone who is a family member or someone with whom you are intimately involved, it is called domestic violence. Domestic violence is a relationship issue that is very important to learn about and be able to avoid. Your parents, friends or perhaps even you may have experienced domestic violence.

Domestic violence is a pattern of behavior in which someone tries to gain power and control over an intimate partner or family member. The partners may or may not be married and may or may not be currently living together. It involves various forms of abuse and generally escalates and becomes more severe over time.

Domestic violence can be physical, emotional, sexual or financial. Most frequently the male is the abuser and the female is the victim, however, the opposite can be the case.

Assuming the woman is the victim and the man is the perpetrator, the victim may show some of the following characteristics:

1. Low self-esteem

2. Physical and emotional signs of stress

3. Goes to great lengths to keep the peace

4. Believes things will get better with her partner

5. Often puts up with various types of abuse until the children begin being hurt

6. Believes she can "fix" her partner's behaviors

The perpetrator often will have these characteristics:

1. Low self-esteem

2. Is emotionally immature or jealous

3. Has impulse control problems

4. Does not accept responsibility for his actions

5. Blames his behaviors on his significant other or stress in his life

6. Appears to be a "good guy" when around others

7. Believes it is ok to keep his partner or wife "in line" even though he may sometimes "go too far".

This repeated pattern with domestic violence involves three specific stages. First, the potential victim will realize that tension and stress are building in the perpetrator. He/she may act very irritable and be short tempered.

During the second stage, the actual battering or abuse occurs. The perpetrator may be physically abusive by hitting or throwing things, or threatening or using weapons.

Over time the battering will become more frequent and often times much more severe. It does **not** stop without lengthy treatment and counseling involving learning new ways to deal with their feelings and anger. Sometimes even seeking help does not change this behavior.

The last stage is what is known as the "honeymoon" stage. This occurs after an abusive episode ends and when the perpetrator has calmed down. He will usually apologize for his behavior, beg forgiveness and promise over and over that this will never happen again. He may send flowers to the victim, take her out to dinner and treat her in special ways. This behavior will not last.

Because the victim may truly care for her abuser, she believes what he says and really wants things to be better again, like they were when they fell in love.

At some point the victim may decide to leave the abuser for the safety of her children and herself. There are several things that need to happen.

The following steps should be taken without the perpetrator's knowledge. The victim should:

1. Have a safety plan. This will include when she will leave, how she will leave, what she will take and where she will go.

2. Identify, in advance, several locations that would be safe places for her and her children to stay. This place should be unknown to the abuser.

3. Make a list of emergency phone numbers of safe family members and friends and keep it with you.

4. DO NOT threaten the perpetrator by telling them you are going to leave. The abuser may become violent.

    The time when the victim is trying to leave is the most dangerous time for injury or death to occur.

5. Have copies of all important documents (for herself and her children) including driver's license numbers, birth certificates, Social Security numbers, veteran's service numbers, legal documents,

extra house, car and storage keys, contact numbers of family/ friends and a bag with change of clothes for herself and her children.

She might also want to gather this information about the perpetrator in case she needs it to have this information to apply for benefits or assistance.

Sometimes victims will keep all of the above items at a family member's or friend's house so that they do not have to worry about remembering to take this information at the time they are trying to get away from the abuser.

Most communities will have a safe family abuse shelter or will be able to refer you to one. By calling the police or the 211 phone number, the victim should be able to locate a safe place to stay if they choose not to be with family or friends.

Identifying resources/services in advance of the time you decide to leave is strongly recommended. (See Resources below).

Many victims feel that there is no way they can survive if they leave the perpetrator. Do not allow this thinking to keep you in an unsafe place. There are many, many resources available to assist you through this process. Finding resources is often a matter of asking people for help.

Resources

- Family, friends, teachers, coaches, or counselors
- Hotline Numbers for numerous concerns- www. pleaselive.org/hotlines
- Law enforcement- call 911
- Community information and referral—call 211
- The National Domestic Abuse Hotline: www. thehotline.org-
- Google "local family abuse centers", "local advocacy centers" and/or "child protective services"

Bullying

If you are old enough to be reading this book you have probably experienced bullying at some time or other. Unfortunately, bullying sometimes begins at a very young age (even as early as two years old) and occurs with adults as well.

Bullying may also occur in domestic violence situations discussed above.

Bullying is usually a combination of verbal and physical actions. It is a deliberately hurtful and wounding behavior with the bully having power over the victim. The bullying behaviors may be face-to-face with the victim or may occur through cyberbullying (email, cell or phone messaging, photos, social media sites, etc.)

The bully usually has average or above average self-esteem. The victims are often anxious, overly sensitive and unable to defend themselves or at least feel that they cannot defend themselves.

Some signs that a child may be experiencing bullying include:

1. Possessions being destroyed

2. Unexplained injuries

3. Difficulty eating or sleeping

4. Coming home extremely hungry (the bully may be taking their lunch)

5. Feeling sick or faking an illness

6. Acting out behaviors like running away or skipping school

7. Showing signs of depression or other signs of mental illness

8. Using alcohol or drugs

9. Talking about or attempting to harm oneself (cutting)

10. Talking about or attempting suicide (find more on suicide below).

Signs of someone who may be a bully are kids who:

1. Act aggressively and get into fights

2. Have friends who bully

3. Blame others for their problems and don't accept responsibility for their actions

    There are a variety of ways to stand up to a bully. Sometimes you may need to use an approach several times or try several different approaches to see what is most effective. But remember, you can take charge.

Ways to stop bullying include:

1. Ignore the behavior- the bully wants to get attention by his/her behaviors. If you ignore name calling or other negative behaviors, the bully does not get any benefit from his bullying. (It may be difficult to ignore this behavior, but it is worth it and often the behavior will eventually stop.)

2. Act confidently. Walk with your head up and shoulders back, like you are in charge.

    If you slouch or hang your head or look like a target for a person who bullies, they will continue their threatening behavior.

3. You can tell the bully to stop. A bully is not expecting you to stand up for yourself so when you do stand up, they may decide you are not a good target.

4. You might laugh or make a joke about a comment the bully makes.

5. Stay with your friends. Bullies usually target kids when they are alone. So avoid bathrooms, empty hallways and other places where you might end up alone with the bully. If you get that creepy feeling that you may be in an unsafe place, leave immediately.

6. If you get into a situation where the bully might try to become physical, look for an exit, talk in a loud voice and do anything you can to attract attention. Think about your situation if you are being bullied or fear this might happen. What are some ways you can draw attention to you and seek help? Perhaps throwing a rock through a window?

7. Some people choose to take a self-defense class to learn other ways to defend themselves. If a bully becomes physical, don't hesitate to fight back.

If the bullying occurs by cyberbullying (online bullying), there are some ways to deal with that as well. Some of the ways to deal with bullying that are listed above will also help with cyberbullying. Some helpful steps might include:

1. Do not react to the bully. Even though you may want to respond online, completely ignore the person's text, post or call. Remember, bullies are seeking attention. If they don't get attention from you, they will generally stop bothering you. If you text them that you are going to report them, that is attention to them.

Before you delete the bully's comments, save every text, email, photo or other contact that you receive. You can print these out to have documentation of their behaviors. Be sure that the date of this contact is included on your documentation. Then you should delete the information.

Should you ever need to report someone to the authorities, this documentation will be very valuable.

Gather information about the bully, but don't confront them. If you confront them you are giving them the attention they want. Save *all* information in case you do report them.

If the cyberbullying continues, you will want to block the bully and report them to your service provider.

Sometimes when cyberbullying occurs it spreads quickly to others and can be very uncomfortable and hurtful. Remembering not to react or respond to any of the bullying will help it disappear sooner.

If the bullying does not readily stop, contact an adult you trust. This might be a parent, teacher, coach, or friend. You do not have to fight this alone and sometimes adults are able to intervene and stop the bullying behavior.

If the bullying is coming from another student, your

school should be notified. The school has a responsibility to help stop this behavior.

If the school does not know about the bullying behavior, there is no way they can help stop it.

Resources

- Family, friends, teachers, coaches, or counselors
- School administrators
- Self-defense classes
- Stop Bullying.gov https://www.stopbullying.gov
- Bullying: MedlinePlus https://medlineplus.gov
- Depression Due to Bullying www.dellchildrens.net/Bullying/Help

Harassment

Harassment is usually thought to be an issue in the workplace when someone with power, money and/or connections puts unwanted pressure on someone to perform sexual acts or other uncomfortable activities in order to get a raise, promotion or a special favor. (See more about harassment in Chapter 4, Keeping Your Job".)

Harassment can also occur in a school setting where a professor has power over the students as they issue the students their grades. Keep in mind that harassment can occur in many situations.

The person in power may annoy, pester, tease, threaten or intimidate someone, or make unwanted sexual advances toward someone with whom they are interested. Harassment might also include telling of off-colored jokes or using words that make someone uncomfortable. This is never ok and there are laws against this.

There are many very powerful, influential people who have been accused of harassment and as a result their reputations and careers are ruined.

If you experience harassment anywhere, it is best to first report this to your immediate supervisor, the supervisor of the person harassing and/or the Human Resources Department.

If your immediate supervisor is the one doing the harassing, you may need to go to his/her immediate supervisor.

Be sure you are documenting every behavior you are concerned about, and everything that was said and done in response to your complaint. Be sure to date every piece of documentation and make a second copy of your documentation to keep at home in a safe place, just in case any records get lost or disappear.

The Human Resources Department should have very specific procedures to follow to investigate harassment complaints.

The person to whom you are reporting should take your complaint very seriously. Workplaces and schools should be safe places to be without distraction and concern from other employees or bosses.

Give the person to whom you complained the opportunity to deal appropriately with your complaint. If there is no action taken in a reasonable amount of time (usually a week or two) you may need to consider speaking with an attorney to handle this situation.

There are many online sites with suggestions for avoiding workplace harassment and how to handle it, should it occur. You can google "ways to avoid workplace harassment" to view these sites.

Resources

- the immediate supervisor
- the supervisor of the person harassing
- Human Resources Department
- Harassment legal definition of harassment https://legal-dictionary.thefreedictionary.com/harassment
- Sexual harassment 101: what everyone needs to know/World news https://www.theguardian.com

Human Trafficking

Human trafficking is the buying and selling of people for forced labor and/or sexual exploitation. People involved with human trafficking are not just in "shady" places and poor parts of town. Some of these traffickers are students in schools and will try to involve students who are attending schools so that they can "use" them. Some traffickers hang out in malls.

Females are most often the victims of human trafficking but males may also be targets. Children as young as three may be targeted. Often victims are school aged. Many people who are trafficked are from lower socioeconomic backgrounds.

There are a number of ways that people look for vulnerable targets. This can happen easily in person and by texting or online.

Sometimes traffickers are very subtle in their recruitment. They may go to a mall and watch young girls. They are looking for girls who appear to be insecure, lonely and have low self-esteem. This is another reason it is important to always present yourself as strong and full of confidence instead of appearing weak and needy.

Some of the signs of someone who may be a victim of trafficking are listed below. They may:

1. be disconnected from family, friends, or communities

2. no longer attend school

3. have signs of physical or mental abuse

4. appear fearful or submissive of whom they are with

5. lack personal possessions

6. appear to be deprived of food, water or sleep, or may be staying in unhealthy, unsafe conditions

7. do not appear able to be free to move as they desire

8. are being coached on what to say

Once the trafficker identifies someone they feel is an easy target, they begin to groom them. They might buy them a drink or a meal or even clothing. They are trying to build a connection with their targets.

If a target is lonely, it is easy for the groomer to develop a relationship with them by sending lots of messages to the victim that he "has her back", he is there for her and will take care of her. If the target was raised in an unhealthy family situation or has few friends, these messages may sound like just what they are missing and needing.

Over time as this relationship grows, the trafficker might convince their target to have sex with someone as a way to earn lots of money and meet the approval of the trafficker.

Keep in mind that anything that sounds too good to be true usually is.

[Stop] Those with whom you form relationships should always have your best interest at heart, not just their own.

Resources

- Friends, family, trusted adults
- Law Enforcement—call 911
- https://polarisproject.org/human-trafficking— information on how to avoid becoming a target for human traffickers.
- https://en.wikipedia.org/wiki/List of organizations that combat human trafficking

Mental Illness

Mental illness is a term you hear often but most people don't understand or are scared of. One way to look at the importance of mental illness is to compare it to physical illness.

If you had a broken leg or were in severe physical pain, you would probably immediately seek medical attention. This is often not the case when people are dealing with emotional or psychological pain. They will often hide their pain from others or even deny to themselves that this pain exists.

If you did not receive treatment for a broken leg, you might end up with a major deformity or even be unable to walk again. If emotional issues go untreated, the person may become withdrawn or depressed and not be able to function at school or work, or even around family members.

Sometimes we do not know about physical problems that people are experiencing until they tell us or a doctor. Emotional problems are the same way. If you or your friend is experiencing some sort of physical problem, it would be very important for someone to know about that. The way people get better is to tell someone who can help them find services or treatment.

Emotional problems that are untreated can lead to mental illness which can range from mild to severe. Like physical problems, mental illnesses, if untreated, can lead to more serious problems and can even cause the person to contemplate or commit suicide. (See section below on suicide.)

Since people are often hesitant to talk about their emotional situations or feelings, it is important to look at their behaviors for signs of concern.

Some things to be aware of are changes that are major, out of proportion, and/or last for several weeks or a month. There are signs listed below that would be concerns. These concerns should be taken even more seriously if someone has just experienced a major life event, like the death of a parent or friend, loss of a relationship or job or any other significant event like failing a grade or getting in trouble with the law.

Some signs to watch for would be:

1. Unnecessary or prolonged anxiety

2. Depression

3. Abrupt weight loss or gain

4. Abrupt change in mood or behavior

5. Habitually falling below their potential

6. Withdrawing from family and friends

7. Eating and sleeping issues

8. Alcohol and/or drug use to cope with problems

9. Thoughts or attempts at physical harm (including cutting and suicide)

10. Unusual fears

Any of these signs, especially if paired with a significant life event like those mentioned above, require attention.

There are a variety of treatments available for those dealing with an emotional or mental issue. These may include a few sessions of counseling, group therapy, or medication. When the situation is more severe, hospitalization may be considered.

The most important thing is that whether you are dealing with some of these issues yourself, or your friend is, you MUST tell someone and seek help. If someone shares their concerns with you, you must be a good listener! There are many forms of help, but nothing will happen if no one knows about it.

Resources

- Family or friends
- A professional counselor
- Call 211
- Call 911 (if the person is in crisis)
- Self-injury hotline 1-800- DON'T CUT
- Crisis Text Line- Text CONNECT to 741741
- National Suicide Prevention Lifeline— 800-273-8255
- National Alliance of Mental Illness (NAMI)— https://www/nami.org.
- Chapters of NAMI are local, state and national. They provide education, information and services to individuals and families dealing with mental illness.
- Know the Warning Signs/NAMI: National Alliance on Mental Illness https://www.nami.org/ Learn-More/Know-the-Warning-Signs
- Hotline Numbers Directory for various concerns- www.pleaselive.org/hotlines

Suicide

If you remember only one thing out of this book, remember that:

Suicide is a PERMANENT solution to a TEMPORARY

problem. There is always another way out, even though you may not have thought of it yet.

Suicide is a very difficult, painful topic to talk about. However, it is prevalent and most importantly, pre-ventable. By knowing some ways to deal with a person contemplating suicide, you may actually save a life by getting this person help.

Many people have thought off-handedly and very briefly that maybe suicide would be the answer to their problems. Fortunately, this is usually a very brief, fleeting thought and the person in crisis will choose another way to deal with their issues.

Suicide may be something you have thought about yourself. PLEASE keep in mind the first sentence in this topic. Suicide is a **permanent** solution to a **temporary** problem.

You may be feeling helpless and hopeless, but there is always more than one way to solve a problem. You may not be able to consider options clearly right now because of your feelings. But remember, there is *always* someone you can reach out to who wants to help you solve your problems.

Below are some things to consider if you or someone else is the person considering suicide. Please think about the following and reach out to someone before acting on your feelings.

1. There is someone who can help. Think about your friends, family members, preacher, youth minister, coaches, teachers, counselors, and any others who are in your life. Any of these individuals would want to help, if they knew you needed it.

2. TELL this person how you are feeling. Be honest.

3. There are many solutions to all problems, but suicide is not a good one. Remember, suicide is a permanent solution to a temporary problem. Ask someone to help you consider other solutions to your problems.

4. Time does pass and over time, feelings will soften.

Talk to yourself or your friend and say some of the things below:

1. What is the worst thing that can happen if I talk to someone?

2. In the morning, things will look different.

3. Tomorrow will bring a new perspective.

4. I will get through this.

5. People do care. I don't have to deal with problems by myself.

In order for people to help, they need to know how you are feeling. If you do not have anyone to talk with, you can call the National Suicide Prevention Lifeline at 1-800-273-8255. This hotline is open 24/7 and is free and confidential. You will also find additional resources listed at the end of this topic.

There are many risk factors for suicide. Some of these are:

1. Family history of suicide

2. Previous suicide attempts

3. Having a specific plan to commit suicide

4. Family issues (losses or abuse)

5. Anniversary of a previous traumatic event

6. Recent loss of parent

7. Depression, moodiness or severe mental illness

8. Drug and/or alcohol abuse or relapse

9. Experiencing hopelessness and helplessness

10. Living alone and being cut off from others.

Signs that should increase the concern that someone might attempt suicide would include:

1. A specific, detailed plan of how they would attempt suicide

    The more detailed the plan, the more serious the threat. If someone has thought about the method, location and other specifics about their suicide attempt, they need *immediate* attention. **Do not leave them alone.**

2. Obtaining guns or pills

3. Getting their personal affairs in order

4. Giving away prized possessions

5. Calling people they know but may not have spoken to recently (in a way, telling them good-bye)

6. Displaying a sudden lifting of spirits and positive outlook

Sometimes there are specific situations that occur that lead someone to consider suicide. These situations might include:

1. Being expelled from school or losing a job

2. Making a recent, unwanted move

3. Losing a major relationship

4. Experiencing the death of a spouse, child, close friend, pet or parent (especially if that person committed suicide).

5. Diagnosis of serious or terminal illness

6. Having sudden, unexpected loss of freedom and fear of punishment

7. Losing financial security

So now you know things that might contribute to why someone may be considering suicide. So, what next?

First of all, if you are feeling nervous thinking about trying to discuss suicide, know that most people do get very nervous when discussing this topic. Many adults and professionals are also very uneasy about discussing suicide. **Talking about suicide will not cause someone to commit suicide.** They are already thinking about it and you will not be putting ideas in their head.

To help with this nervousness I have included questions below that you can ask (if you feel you want to) and some questions not to ask.

If you decide you want to talk with your friend or family member about suicide, or want to talk about your own suicidal feelings, try to find a quiet, private place where you can talk openly with this person. Don't be rushed.

If you are still uncomfortable discussing your concerns with your friend, you can still be a good listener. Let them know you are listening by nodding your head, repeating what they say and asking questions. The important thing is that you are there with your friend and not ignoring them.

There are some indirect ways to ask about suicide. For instance,

1. Are you OK?

2. "Have you been unhappy lately?" or,

3. "You seem to be unhappy."

Some more direct questions might be:

1. "Have you ever been so unhappy you are thinking about ending your life?

2. "Do you ever wish you could go to sleep and never wake up?

3. "You look pretty miserable. Are you feeling miserable?" or

4. "When people are upset, as you seem to be, they sometimes wish they were dead. I'm wondering if you are feeling this way."

If you feel you cannot ask these questions, Do NOT worry or feel badly. Stay with your friend until you can get an adult to help you with the situation. Let them know you are going to stay with them until help arrives. *Do not leave them alone.*

If you are concerned about your friend being suicidal, don't let them convince you that they are ok. Sometimes once someone has a plan to commit suicide they appear to feel better and they will try to convince you that they are fine.

So you might say to your friend, "I am worried about you. I want to get you help. Let's go talk to the coach" (or some other trusted available adult).

Some things NOT to say to someone contemplating suicide might be:

1. "You wouldn't do anything stupid or crazy like that, would you?"

     Remember, this person is not thinking as you are. They are emotionally distraught and cannot think reasonably.

2. "You are joking, aren't you? Surely you aren't serious."

3. "Well, just go ahead and do it then."

These are not helpful comments.

It is critical to discuss the topic of suicide with a person you fear may be suicidal instead of ignoring the possibility. BUT IT IS NOT CRITICAL THAT YOU BE THE ONE TO DISCUSS THIS.

Remember, someone who is considering suicide is not thinking logically. They are feeling very helpless and hopeless. They are emotionally unhealthy at this moment.

In some cases there is nothing ANYONE can do

to prevent someone from committing suicide. It is no one else's fault.

So, decide who you are going to talk with, call or text them and BE HONEST!

Resources

- National Suicide Prevention Lifeline at 1-800-273-8255.
- Crisis Text Line- Text CONNECT to 741741
- Hotline numbers for numerous specific concerns- www.pleaselive.org/hotlines

Alcohol

Alcohol and drugs are very prevalent in our society. Your parents or other adults you know may consume alcohol. That does not mean that the use of alcohol is good for you or something you should use. But at some point you will need to make choices about whether or not you will try alcohol and/or drugs. Remember, **you** are in charge of your decisions.

You may frequently be asked or encouraged by your friends to try alcohol or drugs. The information below will help you make an informed decision about whether or not you are going to use alcohol or drugs.

Let's talk about alcohol first. Someone may want to drink to be part of a social group. Maybe many of their friends are drinking and they want to be included and popular.

Others find that by drinking alcohol they can temporarily escape their worries or problems. The downside is that when the alcohol has left their systems and they are sober again, the problems are still there to be solved. Alcohol has only served as a temporary escape.

One of the effects of alcohol on the body is that it slows down the central nervous system resulting in people feeling more relaxed and less inhibited. If someone has difficulty meeting people or talking in crowds, the alcohol may help relax them. Another effect can be that they behave in ways they regret once they sober up.

When someone drinks alcohol it affects many parts of the body. It can affect your heart, liver, and the pancreatitis. Another important part of the body that is affected is the brain. Alcohol particularly impacts judgment and thinking.

CAUTION

Some people think their judgment is affected only when they are drunk, but any amount of alcohol will go to the brain and affect one's judgment to some degree.

Alcohol also causes people to have lowered self-control, a feeling of well-being and to think that they are more adequate than they actually are.

Drinking too much alcohol can cause one to experience blackouts (not remembering where they have been, what they did or how they got home), and withdrawal from the alcohol leaving their system.

Withdrawal may include headaches, vomiting, anxiety, heart palpitations and seizures. In some cases it can lead to death.

If you are planning to have an evening with friends, regardless of your age, and decide to drink alcohol, ALWAYS have a designated driver who agrees to not drink any alcohol. This person agrees that they will remain sober and drive everyone to their destination at the end of the evening. This is a very important responsibility and you must always keep this commitment if you agree to become a designated driver.

If you realize the person you have trusted to be a designated driver has decided to drink, always call a parent or friend or hire someone like an Uber driver to see that you get home safely.

Excessive drinking over a short period of time can cause alcohol poisoning. If someone you are with appears to have passed out due to drinking alcohol, get them immediate attention (even if you and the drinker are under the legal age to drink). Someone experiencing alcohol poisoning appears to have passed out, but their condition is really much more serious. You might very likely save their life by getting immediate medical attention.

You may have heard about situations where people are forced to drink a large amount of alcohol over a very short time. Sometimes this is related to hazing that may occur at a party or at a group setting. A common situation in which this occurs is when fraternity members are hazing their pledges. If you get in a situation where someone is trying to force you to consume large quantities of alcohol, remember, you have a choice. You DO NOT have to do this. Saying no in a pressure situation is better than losing your life.

Sometimes people have information about alcohol that may be incorrect. Below are some facts about alcohol that are important to know.

1. Alcohol is not a stimulant. It is classified as a depressant because it slows down the central nervous system.

2. Drinking coffee does not sober you up.

3. You will often not have signs that you are drunk, but your judgment and thinking are already affected.

4. Intoxication is not greater when you mix beer and liquor. How intoxicated you become is based on the alcoholic content of the drinks you consume.

5. Some people think you cannot become an alcoholic by drinking only beer. This is not correct.

One of the causes of someone becoming an alcoholic is that they have an inherited genetic predisposition to alcohol. If alcoholism runs in your family, you may have inherited this predisposition. This does not mean that you will automatically become an alcoholic. If you never drink alcohol, the predisposition will not be triggered.

If there is alcoholism in your family, deciding to drink is a very serious decision. Some alcoholics have become addicted from their first use of alcohol. Other people have been drinking over a period of time before problems from drinking begin. The real issue is that you don't know when problems with alcohol will start. Once the problems begin, you will see issues with your health, job and relationships. The end result may be addiction.

Once a person is addicted, it is strongly recommended that they go into treatment to deal with their addiction. This can be a long, expensive and painful process. Some people are in treatment multiple times before they are successfully in recovery.

There are Alcoholics Anonymous (AA) groups in almost all locations that support someone who is recovering. The groups meet at various times and in various locations. Some are closed groups in which only members may attend and some are open to visitors. There are both smoking and non-smoking groups. There may be several groups to choose from in your community, so there should be one that fits everyone's needs.

Alanon is a support group for the family members of

someone dealing with alcoholism. The family members often attend their meeting at the same time an AA meeting is being held.

A very serious concern about teens drinking is that the human brain continues to develop until someone reaches the age of 25-28. If someone starts drinking prior to that age, this can seriously affect the development of their brain. It can also affect the emotional development of a teen.

As you are thinking about the choices you are going to make, keep in mind that the age to legally drink alcohol is 21. If you decide to drink prior to 21 and are caught by law enforcement, you may have the beginning of a criminal record. This record can affect your ability to get jobs, your reputation and your relationships for the rest of your life.

Resources

- https://www.niaaa.nih.gov/alcohol-health/alcohols-effects-body
- National Institute on Drug Abuse (NIDA), https://www.drugabuse.gov/drugs-abuse
- https://medineplus.gov> Health Topics
- AA- Alcoholics Anonymous- a fellowship for men and women who have had a drinking problem. It is international and a highly recommended support group for those in recovery from addiction. The Alcoholics Anonymous group work uses a twelve step program as its foundation.

- By calling 211, you should be able to find the meeting locations of these groups in your community.

Drugs

Deciding to try illegal drugs is a very, very serious issue with major consequences. For many people, the reasons they try drugs are similar to the reasons they try alcohol.

People who end up addicted to drugs never thought they would become addicted when they decided to try various kinds of drugs.

Sometimes people will "slip" drugs into others drinks or food. If you are out in public and leave your food or drink unattended to visit with others or go to the restroom, do not continue consuming that drink or food.

If you realize you have left your drink pour it out in the restroom or into a nearby plant. Start with a fresh drink.

The addictive effects of many over-the-counter pain killers and illegal street drugs are a huge concern. Most people who decide to try drugs think that they will not become addicted. They can't see themselves being involved with drug dealers or shooting up in crack houses. For many users, this is where they can end up very quickly.

There are several classifications of drugs. Stimulants speed up the central nervous system; depressants slow down the central nervous system. Hallucinogens cause hallucinations and delusions. Psychotropic drugs are used mainly to treat mental illness.

There is a great deal of information about the various drugs and their effects but it is too much information to detail here. I have listed resources at the end of this section.

If you are curious, I would encourage you to access the National Institutes of Health (NIH) website at https://search.nih.gov/ for the topics you are wondering about. Also the National Institute on Drug Abuse (NIDA), https://www.drugabuse.gov/drugs-abuse is an excellent website.

Many of the drugs are highly addictive. It can become extremely difficult, painful and expensive to go through treatment to become clean from these drugs.

Keep in mind that the legal consequences from using illegal substances may be much greater than from the use of alcohol. If you are using or selling drugs, and receive a conviction for using or selling, prison time may be for years.

Long term effects on your health can also be major and lifelong.

Using illegal drugs should be avoided at all costs. There is no positive reason to use illegal drugs or are there any positive effects from using them.

If pain killers are prescribed to you by a doctor, discuss the possible effects at length.

If alcoholism or drug addiction runs in your family, be sure to let your medical provider know about the family history before using the medications. It is possible you could have inherited the predisposition to addiction. The prescribed medications may lead to addiction. (See more information in the topic above-Alcohol).

Resources

- National Institutes of Health (NIH) https://search.nih.gov/
- National Institute on Drug Abuse (NIDA), https://www.drugabuse.gov/drugs-abuse
- NA—Narcotics Anonymous- This is a twelve step recovery group similar to AA (see the description above). It operates in the same format as AA. By calling 211, you should be able to find the meeting locations.

Sex and Pregnancy

Among other issues that people deal with as they are on the road to independence is how they will handle their sexuality. This is another area in which you are in charge of your behaviors.

Hormones are raging as you mature, you may become infatuated with others and relationships may move to new levels.

There is a lot to learn about your own physical and emotional development. You may be lucky enough to know someone you trust to talk with about sexuality. But for many people this is an awkward, uncomfortable topic and is never addressed.

Many teens receive their information about sexuality and pregnancy from friends. These friends have good intentions, but are often misinformed. For example, some people think you cannot become pregnant if you have sexual intercourse standing up. This is WRONG!!

Identify a family member, doctor, pastor, youth minister or someone else with whom you can discuss questions you might have about sexuality. If you cannot think of someone you would like to talk with about these questions, a good website to visit is http://www.everydayhealth.com/sexual-health.

Some people also have questions regarding their sexual identity. There are a number of websites that can address these questions also. One of these sites is https://www.uofmhealth.org/health-library/abj9665.

Many people have talked about and thought about sexuality prior to puberty. They have thought about the pros and cons of sexual intercourse and have made a conscious decision to not have sexual intercourse prior to marriage. This is a very mature decision, and very smart in terms of preventing pregnancy prior to marriage or the development of a life-long relationship.

Other people, in the heat of the moment of sexual activity, may feel that if they take precautions to prevent pregnancy, they do not need to worry about becoming pregnant. They then allow their relationship to progress to having sexual intercourse.

Even though you use precautions, pregnancies can still occur. Sometimes people forget to take birth control pills, or products intended to prevent pregnancy are defective.

Some causes of teen and early pregnancy are lack of education and information about reproduction, peer pressure, excessive drinking, experimenting with drugs, and media influence that makes pregnancy and caring for a baby appear glamourous.

Young mothers often are forced to drop out of school to care for their babies. They often lose contact with their friends. It is difficult for teen moms to complete their own development. They must now focus on their baby's needs instead of their own development and schooling. A baby can also put a strain on relationships with the father. Needed financial resources to care for her baby may not be available.

Early pregnancy (while a girl is still maturing) can be very hazardous to her health as well as to the baby's health. If a girl becomes pregnant prior to 15 the risk of anemia, high blood pressure, low birth weight in her baby, premature birth or infant mortality can occur. There may also be difficulties with labor and delivery as the girl's body is not as mature as it needs to be to handle pregnancy.

Teens who become sexually active may fail to think about all of the possible consequences. In addition to those mentioned above, there is the risk of contracting sexually transmitted diseases (STDs). Sexually transmitted diseases are passed from one person to another through sexual contact. Sometimes the person who has the disease is not aware they have it and unknowingly passes it to their sexual partner(s).

You may have heard about some of these diseases that can be passed to another through sexual activity. They include HIV, chlamydia, gonorrhea, genital herpes, and human papillomavirus (HPV). By checking websites you may obtain a great deal of information about these various diseases. One reliable site is http://www.cdc.gov/healthyyouth/sexualbehaviors.

In most areas there are local, state and national agencies that can help pregnant women with education on pregnancy, child birth and parenting. There are usually agencies that can help provide car seats, baby beds, diapers and food, if needed. By goggling your state name and the word "pregnancy" you should be able to find a number of helpful resources in your location.

In some situations, the teen mother may decide that it is in her baby's and her best interest to place her child for adoption. There are a number of families who are interested in adoption. If this is the decision you have made, be sure to find an adoption agency that is licensed so that you and your baby can receive the best quality of services.

Google adoption agencies in your hometown and you should find a number of approved agencies that handle adoptions. Most states have networks of agencies that work with young moms. In Texas you can google texaspregnancy.org to identify services in the state. Most states will have a similar site.

Resources

- Call 211 for local resources
- http://www.everydayhealth.com/sexual-health.
- https://www.uofmhealth.org/health-library/abj9665.

13

*Developing Interpersonal
Communication and
Problem Solving Skills*

*I am convinced that life is 10 percent what happens to me
and 90 percent of how I react to it.*

—Charles Bukowski

This book has discussed many of the challenges that people face as they are navigating the road to independence and learning to live on their own. There will be other bumps and holes in the road that you will encounter on your journey, but the good news is that there are some tools and techniques to help manage these challenges. Below are some very helpful and easy

to use tools you may find useful as you are address-
ing some of the issues dealt with in other chapters.
Communication skills are also discussed in Chapter 4,
Keeping Your Job.

Communication

How we communicate with others can help us solve
problems, meet new people, develop friendships and
be successful and respected in our interpersonal situations. Or, it can cause confusion, misunderstanding or
get us in trouble.

There are some very basic communication skills that
are easy to learn and apply. Keep in mind that these
skills work with friends, parents, teachers, employers
and anyone else with whom you talk.

First of all, learn to be a good listener. This sounds very
basic, and is, but often people do not practice these
techniques. A good listener will maintain eye contact
with the person to whom they are talking. They will
nod occasionally as the person is talking and will peri-
odically comment on something that the other person
has said. Asking questions related to the topic of conversation is also helpful.

DO NOT CHECK YOUR PHONE OR TEXT when some-
one is trying to have a conversation with you, no matter
who this person is. What they are saying is important to
them and it is important that you respect that. Do not
interrupt or cut-off the person who is talking.

Next, you must be a good responder. Reply to the topic that the other person is sharing, do not change the subject to yourself. Try to connect with the person's feelings.

You might say, "It sounds like you are feeling_____ (sad). " Or, I am wondering if you are_____ (unhappy)." You can fill in these blanks with whatever positive or negative word fits your situation.

Listen to the feelings behind the words that the person is saying so that you can "connect" with them. Do they have other feelings that they are not mentioning? State or reword what the person said to be sure you are correctly understanding this person.

There are actually four parts to communication. They are the sender, message, channel and receiver. Things can go wrong in any part leading to misunderstanding, confusion and/or hurt feelings.

The "sender" may be having a bad day and is not being pleasant so it is difficult to engage with them. They may not be listening to you.

The "message" includes the verbal and non-verbal parts of what someone is saying. The verbal part is the actual wording. The non-verbal part is any facial expression or body movement that affects the words, like a snarl, rolling of the eyes or shrugging of the shoulders.

The "channel" refers to the way in which the message is sent. Did you communicate through a phone call, text, email or face-to-face. There can be difficulties and misunderstandings that result from any of these forms of communication.

As the "receiver", you may realize that you are tired and are not listening well, or that you have a million things to do and cannot concentrate on a conversation.

One way to check how effective you are as a communicator is to think back on recent conversations you had in which there was a misunderstanding. Try to figure out in which part(s) of the communication the problems occurred. Review what you said to see how you may have contributed to the miscommunication.

There are three types of communication, passive, aggressive and assertive. If you are being passive, you are not expressing your feelings or emotions, but simply agreeing with someone else.

If you are aggressive, you may be verbally attacking the other person, saying things like, "you are so stupid", or "why do you feel that way? That is crazy".

An assertive communicator will share their opinions and feelings without verbally attacking the other person or expecting them to agree with you. The goal is to become as assertive in your communications as possible. Think about what you want to say to others without verbally attacking them or making the other person feel defensive.

Pros and Cons Sheet

A pros and cons sheet can be very effective in helping you make important decisions and it is very easy to use.

At the top of a piece of paper write an issue about which you are trying to make a decision. For instance, "Should I go to a community college vs. a four-year institution?" Below that write "Pros" on the left-hand side of the paper and on the right-hand side write "Cons".

Begin listing as many good reasons (pros) for attending a community college as you can think of. On the right-hand side, list the bad reasons (cons) for attending a community college. Usually one list becomes much longer than the other very quickly. Whichever side has the most items is the side that is likely the best decision. If one side does not have more reasons than the other, it may be a situation in which either decision may be a good one.

You will be surprised at how quickly you will be able to make a decision that is made on thoughts and not feelings and emotions.

Thought Cycle

The Thought Cycle is known by several different names. This is a way that you can help yourself look at how your thoughts and feelings may be impacting your behaviors.

On a blank piece of paper, draw a circle. At the top of the circle write the word "thoughts". At the right hand side of the circle write "feelings", at the bottom of the circle write "behaviors" and on the left hand side of the circle write "results".

Let's pretend that you are in school and math is a very difficult subject for you. When you think about your "*thoughts*" related to math, you may think, I am so stupid, I don't understand math, I will never pass this class. If you are thinking this way, it is likely that you will be "*feeling*" inadequate, unable to complete the course, or that you are the only one who doesn't get it.

If you are feeling this way, chances are that when you get to math class you will "freeze up". Your "*behaviors*" in class might be that you will not listen as well, you keep thinking and feeling inadequate and so you become preoccupied with your thoughts and feelings. Another "*behavior*" may be that you miss the explanations that the teacher is giving. You might also lose tract of the problems on which you are supposed to be working.

Now, look at the "*results*". Chances are that since you missed the explanations of the teacher, you will not be successful with your homework and/or exams. If this continues, you really may fail the class.

This exercise points out how critical it is to be aware of your thoughts. And who controls your thoughts? Of course, you do. Here you are, in charge of yourself again. So adjust your *thoughts* (that you are in control of) to something like, "I am going to work hard. I will get a tutor. I will stay after class for more help."

If you are *thinking* this way you are likely to *"feel"* more confident, and capable. This is likely to cause you to *"behave"* differently. You are likely to study more and ask questions in class when you don't understand something. The *"result"* will probably be higher grades. See how important controlling your thinking can be?

One of the most important tools you have to control your behavior (that no one else has or controls for you), is how you think about a situation. Managing your own thoughts by getting rid of negative thoughts and replacing them with positive thoughts is crucial to gaining independence successfully.

Getting rid of negative thoughts and replacing those negative thoughts with positive thoughts may take some practice. You may find you need to remind yourself that you are thinking negatively. Maybe you put a note on your mirror that you see when you wake up in the morning saying, "Today is going to be a great day!", or "Think positively!".

Some people wear a rubber band on their wrists and when they think negatively, they pop the rubber band as a reminder to change their thinking to something positive. You might also consider asking a friend to re-mind you to think positively if they hear you speaking negatively.

Changing your thinking might take several weeks or a month, but it can definitely happen. It re-quires that you take charge of your thoughts.

Problem Solving

Some situations that need resolution require more effort that using the Pros/Cons Sheet or the Thought Cycle. The following approach requires several steps but can be very helpful in identifying ways a problem may be solved.

This particular problem solving approach has several parts to it. They are as follows:

- Step 1. State the problem clearly.
- Step 2. Generate possible solutions.
- Step 3. Determine possible consequences to each of the possible solutions.
- Step 4. Select a solution.
- Step 5. Implement the solution.
- Step 6. Evaluate the solution.

At any point in this approach you may realize that what you thought was the original problem is actually not, that it is something else. This is part of the value of this approach. If you do not clearly define the problem, any-thing you do to try to solve it will not be effective. If you decide you do not have the problem correctly defined, return to Step 1, restate the problem as you now view it and then work through the other steps that follow.

To demonstrate this approach, let's assume that you have a roommate who will not clean up after herself.

- Step 1. The problem is that Jenny will not clean up after herself, leaving the apartment a wreck.
- Step 2. Possible solutions-
    a. clean up the apartment myself
    b. hire someone to do this
    c. talk to Jenny about this
    d. throw all of her things away
    e.   get another roommate

(Be sure to write down *any* possible solution even if it is totally unrealistic.)

- Step 3. Determine possible consequences to each of the above possible solutions. Cross off the ones that won't work or you don't like.
    a. I will be doing all of the work and Jenny will not do her part.
    b. I cannot afford to pay someone to do this.
    c. She would understand my feelings if I communicate this correctly and would probably be willing to clean up her items.
    d. Jenny would probably get mad, expect me to pay for her items, ruin a great friendship
    e. I don't know of anyone else to room with and I like Jenny a lot

- Step 4. As you look at the consequences you have written, strike through the ones that you do not like. As you see, the best consequence becomes clear.

- Step 5. Now you can decide when you will talk to Jenny, how you will word your feelings, and decide exactly what you would like Jenny to do (clean up every Saturday, every day, etc.)
  You may decide together that each evening you will ask Jenny to clean up and she agrees to do it at that time.

- Step 6. Set a time when you will evaluate your plan. Will you review it in one week, once a month, etc., to determine if this approach is working or not? If it is not, you will need to decide if you are really working on the correct problem, or if you need to generate other possible solutions.

By working through this approach to problem solving, you will find that you are being much more objective than emotional in reaching an effective solution.

Resources

- https://www.smartsheet.com/problem-solving techniques

- https://kvanb.com/how-to-solve-personal-probems-in-life/

- https://www.positivityblog.com/how-to-solve-a-problem-6-quick-and-powerful-tips/

Conclusion

You are now equipped with many tips and techniques to help you navigate your own journey to independence. Additional resources that expand on each of the particular topics discussed in this book may be found on the internet, at libraries, and in book stores.

Friends, relatives, neighbors, and professionals are also available to help you navigate the road to independence.

I wish you the very best on your journey!

CPSIA information can be obtained
at www.ICGtesting.com
Printed in the USA
LVHW032120011220
673137LV00004B/698

9 781604 942514